Cultivating Habits for a Happier & Healthier Life

Do it every day

SUSHIL KUMAR

BLUEROSE PUBLISHERS
India | U.K.

Copyright © Dr. Sushil Kumar 2025

All rights reserved by author. No part of this publication may be reproduced, stored in a retrieval system or transmitted in any form or by any means, electronic, mechanical, photocopying, recording or otherwise, without the prior permission of the author. Although every precaution has been taken to verify the accuracy of the information contained herein, the publisher assume no responsibility for any errors or omissions. No liability is assumed for damages that may result from the use of information contained within.

BlueRose Publishers takes no responsibility for any damages, losses, or liabilities that may arise from the use or misuse of the information, products, or services provided in this publication.

For permissions requests or inquiries regarding this publication, please contact:

BLUEROSE PUBLISHERS
www.BlueRoseONE.com
info@bluerosepublishers.com
+91 8882 898 898
+4407342408967

ISBN: 978-93-6452-207-6

Cover design: Daksh
Typesetting: Tanya Raj Upadhyay

First Edition: March 2025

INTRODUCTION

If you want to be better than you were yesterday, doing certain things every day can help you improve. First, think about what you are thankful for and try to be positive. Take care of yourself by exercising, relaxing, and doing things you enjoy. Make goals you can reach and work on them little by little. Believe that you can learn and grow from challenges. Be nice to others and make connections with them. Learn from what goes well and what does not, and use that to help you in the future. Do things that make you think and be creative. Doing these things every day will help you get better bit by bit.

"Do it every day" aims to bring your attention to your daily routine. It also suggests ways to be more productive by adjusting your daily schedule a little bit. As a result, you will be more energetic, positive, and optimistic. "Do it every day" guides you to adopt a path toward a successful and happy life by making small, and dedicated efforts.

"Do it every day" asks you about the things you do every day. At the end of every chapter, there is a worksheet for you to fill out with your own answers. Do not forget to write in this book.

TABLE OF CONTENTS

CHAPTER 1: WAKE UP EARLY 1
CHAPTER 2: EXERCISE 5
CHAPTER 3: EAT ONE HEALTHY MEAL 10
CHAPTER 4: DRINK ENOUGH WATER 14
CHAPTER 5: WORK ON YOUR HOBBY 19
CHAPTER 6: READ AN INSPIRATIONAL QUOTE 22
CHAPTER 7: REDUCE SCREEN TIME 26
CHAPTER 8: SET A GOAL FOR TODAY 30
CHAPTER 9: BE CONSISTENT 33
CHAPTER 10: PLAY A SPORT 37
CHAPTER 11: SPEND TIME WITH YOURSELF 41
CHAPTER 12: HAVE ENOUGH SLEEP 45
CHAPTER 13: VISUALIZATION 48
CHAPTER 14: ENCOURAGE YOURSELF 54
CHAPTER 15: RECOGNIZE THE TIME WASTERS 59
CHAPTER 16: STOP OVERTHINKING 64
CHAPTER 17: READ BOOKS 68
CHAPTER 18: WRITE SOMETHING 71
CHAPTER 19: WATCH YOUR THOUGHTS 75
CHAPTER 20: FOCUSED TOWARD YOUR GOALS 80
CHAPTER 21: POSITIVE ATTITUDE 85
CHAPTER 22: CHALLENGE YOURSELF 90
CHAPTER 23: TAKE IMMEDIATE ACTION 95
CHAPTER 24: LISTEN MUSIC 99

CHAPTER 25: WORK ON YOUR SKILL 103
CHAPTER 26: LEARN SOMETHING NEW EVERY DAY 107
CHAPTER 27: TRACK YOUR PROGRESS 110
CHAPTER 28: DO A LITTLE MORE 114
REFERENCES.. 119

CHAPTER 1:
WAKE UP EARLY

"Some people dream of success, while other people get up every morning and make it happen"

- Wayne Huizenga

If you look at successful people around the world in any area of life, they all are early risers.

Tim Cook, CEO of Apple, wakes up at 3:45 A.M.

Pepsico CEO, Indra Nooyi, wakes up at 4 A.M.

Dwayne Johnson wakes up at 4 A.M.

Howard Schultz, CEO of Starbucks, and CEO of Disney, Bob Iger are also early risers.

Waking up early is a good idea because it can make you more productive and help you feel better. People who wake up early have more time for things they enjoy, like exercising, meditating, eating a relaxed breakfast, or planning a day ahead. This can make rest of the day feel nicer. Early mornings are quiet, which gives a relaxing environment to focus on your day ahead it. Also, waking up early can help you sleep better by keeping your body's internal clock in check. It can also make you feel accomplished and in control of your day.

Now you might be thinking about yourself and the excuses you make like, not having enough time or wishing you had more. So ask yourself, how can you make more time? Obviously by taking a closer look at your day. Pay attention to your daily activities; identify the areas where you can create more time? You will surely find many areas.

Getting up early is a helpful habit that can make you:

- More productive and happier.

- Set a positive tone for the whole day.
- Can improve your sleep quality by synchronizing your body's internal clock.
- Give you a sense of achievement and control over your day.

People find it difficult to wake up early, but it is easier if they sleep early. You must sleep between 10 to 11 PM to wake up early. You can adjust this time according to your schedule. In a study, it is discovered that our brain produces a chemical called melatonin which helps in sleeping. It production increases when you sleep every day at the same time.

About a month ago, when I was thinking about writing a first chapter on waking up early, I came across a story about a YouTuber who initially struggled to wake up early. He tried his best to set an alarm that required him to solve some puzzles to wake up. He also hired a person, but nothing worked out. Until he found a reason to wake up early. I also have a similar story how I made myself an early riser. I hired a personal gym trainer to wake me up at 5:30 A.M So I was able to reach gym at 6:00 o'clock every morning.

You can utilize it to work on your most ambitious goal. Set aside specific time intervals each day. This could be as little as 30 minutes per day. Set some measures and track the improvements per week. For example, if you want to learn typing, measure how many words you type per minute.

You can find more time by turning your phone off or set it to silent, find a peaceful place and concentrate exclusively on your goal. To stay organized and track your progress, use tools such as to-do lists and planners. you can also set deadlines for each work to ensure accountability and motivation. Celebrate small wins along the way to keep your spirit high.

Waking up early is easy but it can be tough for those who are late risers. However, starting by sleeping 30 minutes earlier than you usually do, can do miracles. If you are ready, then ask yourself to make new change to your daily wake up schedule.

Finally, you have extra time you have been looking for. You can use this time to make a fortune. You can invest it into your hobbies you are passionate about. You could work on playing some instrument, preparing a TED talk, writing a book, drawing a painting, creating or composing music etc.

So, Set an alarm now and answer these questions.

Ask yourself,

1. What would be the time for me to go to bed from now?

2. What would be the best time for me to wake up?

3. What is the reason to wake up early?

Be honest to yourself while answering the above questions. Don't be in hurry to write answers, as a worksheet has been attached at the end of this chapter.

However, the key points to remember from this chapter are:

- Waking up early is a habit of many successful people
- More time for yourself (exercise, meditation, hobbies, planning)
- Improved focus and productivity (quiet mornings)
- Better sleep quality (regulated body clock)
- Feeling of accomplishment and control
- Gradually adjust your sleep schedule
- Sleep early to wake up early (aim for 10-11pm)
- Find your motivation and a reason to get out of bed early
- Use your extra time for hobbies, passions, and personal goals (learning a skill, writing, playing music)
- Track your progress and celebrate milestones to stay motivated.

Worksheet: Wake Up Early

1. What would be the time for me to go to bed from now?

----

2. What would be the best time for me to wake up?

----

3. What is the reason to wake up early?

CHAPTER 2: EXERCISE

"Take care of your body. It's the only place you have to live"

- Jim Rohn

Exercising in the morning can be a great way to start your day with energy and get a variety of health benefits. As a fitness enthusiast, I have applied a daily routine for exercise. You don't need to become a gym fellow overnight. Start with small, simple exercises like a:

- 15-minute walk each day.
- Use stair case.
- Doing aerobics.
- Stretching

As you get stronger, you can gradually increase the time or intensity. Remember, even a little bit of exercise is better than none! Daily exercise for 30-40 minutes can really boost up your confidence level, improve your mood and skin health, control your weight, reduce stress, and improve your cognitive skills. According to a research published in *Korean Journal of Family Medicine* shows that people who are physically inactive have a higher risk of death as compared to actively engaged in physical activities.

What you can do?

- You can start your day by drinking a glass of water to rehydrate your body after a night's sleep.
- Setting a schedule for a workout helps you to establish a habit. You can setup according to your daily routine, either in the morning or evening.

- The type of exercise you do, vary depending on your preferences and goals.
- Begin with a light warm-up to prepare your body for more intense exercise. This can include stretching, yoga, or a short walk.
- If you're not already a morning person, you may need to adjust your sleep schedule to wake up earlier. Gradually shift your bedtime and wake-up time to ensure you get enough sleep.

It is easy to follow the above suggestions. To make it even easier, consider preparing your workout clothes and equipment the night before to remove any morning hurdles. You can also stay motivated by creating an inspiring playlist, exercising with a friend, or setting fitness goals to track your progress. After your morning workout, rehydrate with water or enjoy a healthy post-workout snack. Have a nutritious breakfast that includes protein, carbohydrates, and healthy fats to refuel your body after exercise. Try to make it a daily habit or at least five times a week.

However, if you are thinking after reading above paragraphs that exercise is only good for physical health. You are really missing the important aspect: mental health. Mental health is actually the most important one. Doing physical workout releases a hormone called endorphins that helps in dealing with pain.

According a research title "Health Benefits of Exercise", regular exercise can delay upto 40 chronic diseases to name some common diseases, like Constipation, Depression and anxiety, Coronary heart disease, Stroke, Hypertension, Obesity, Osteoporosis, Fatty liver, Diabetes, Breast and Colon cancer etc.

I started my exercise journey in September 2021 and joined a nearby gym. Before that I was fitness enthusiast but not regular with my exercise schedule. It's been more than three years now, I am regularly exercising for 30-40 minutes daily. My workout routine starts with a short walk for 15 minutes, followed by stretching and jumping jacks (3 rep of 10). After that, I do 30 push ups in one go. Then I do plank for 1 to 1.5 minutes. Finally, end with "savasana", which is a relaxing pose, where you close your eyes, breathe deeply, and focus on letting go of all tension and stress in your body and mind. The goal is to be completely still and relaxed, as if you are taking a restful nap, allowing your body to rejuvenate and your mind to become calm and peaceful.

This routine energizes me to start my day with full of confidence. Over time, I have developed a habit of exercising daily.

Now it's your turn to make it a habit and win over laziness, poor body language, negative thoughts, overthinking, and procrastination. Start today, do it every day. Let's do a simple breathing exercise to start with. Sit straight, take a deep breath. Hold it for 10 seconds, and release slowly. Feel the air leaving your nostrils. Yes, you are right. I know, "How are you feeling right now." "RELAXED!"

You can repeat it for at least five times whenever you feel little bit off and lazy during work. It will take less than two minutes.

Ask yourself,

1. What would be the best time for me to do exercise?

2. Which type of exercise I can start with?

3. What would be my exercise routine?

To make maximum benefits after asking above questions to yourself. Write the honest answer in the worksheet given at the end of this chapter and read it at least three times. After that you will find yourself more motivated and enthusiastic to start a new exercise journey.

However, the key points to remember from this chapter are:
- Begin with small, achievable goals like a 15-minute walk, and gradually increase time or intensity as you build strength.
- Drink a glass of water first thing in the morning to rehydrate.

- Establish a regular workout routine that fits your daily schedule, whether in the morning or evening.
- Pick exercises based on your preferences and goals.
- Lay out exercise clothes and equipment the night before to reduce morning obstacles.
- Use a motivating playlist, work out with a friend, or set fitness goals to keep on track.
- Rehydrate and have a nutritious breakfast with protein, carbohydrates, and healthy fats.
- Exercise releases endorphins, which help manage pain and improve mental health.
- Regular exercise can delay or prevent chronic diseases like heart disease, diabetes, and depression.
- An example routine includes walking, stretching, jumping jacks, push-ups, planks, and ending with "savasana" for relaxation.

Worksheet: Exercise

1. What would be the best time for me to do exercise?

----

2. Which type of exercise I can start with?

----

3. What would be my exercise routine?

CHAPTER 3:
EAT ONE HEALTHY MEAL

"About eighty percent of the food on shelves of supermarkets today didn't exist 100 years ago."

— Larry McCleary

You can make a big difference in your health by eating one healthy meal every day. A healthy, well-balanced diet gives your body the nutrients it needs to stay healthy, provide energy, and boost your immune system. Eating a range of food groups, like fruits, veggies, lean proteins, and whole grains, makes sure that your body gets all the vitamins, minerals, and antioxidants it needs to stay healthy.

Starting your day with a healthy breakfast can establish a good tone for the rest of the day. Breakfast is generally referred to as the most essential meal of the day, and with good reason. It provides the energy and focus required to complete tasks with clarity and efficiency. A meal high in fiber and protein helps to manage blood sugar levels, reducing energy dumps and cravings later on. For example, oatmeal with fresh berries and a side of yogurt gives a well-balanced mix of carbohydrates, protein, and healthy fats to keep you going all morning.

A healthy meal can also boost cognitive function and mood. The brain requires a consistent supply of nourishment to function properly. Foods high in omega-3 fatty acids, such as salmon and walnuts, promote brain health, improve mental clarity, and reduce feelings of stress and anxiety. Also, the complex carbs in healthy grains and vegetables helps in keeping blood sugar levels steady, which lowers the risk of mood swings and irritation.

Making conscious choices about what to eat helps you have a good relationship with food and helps you focus on your long-term health goals. For example, a colorful salad with lots of different veggies for lunch gives you important nutrients that keep you motivated for the task. Preparation and having a healthy meal may also be a mindful activity that makes you value the food you eat.

The benefits of eating well extend beyond physical health. Good nutrition enhances your emotional and psychological well-being. Sharing a nourishing meal with loved ones fosters connections and strengthens relationships, contributing to a sense of fulfilment and happiness. Whether it's cooking a meal together, enjoying a family dinner, or having a potluck with friends, the social aspect of eating can be just as important as the nutritional content of the food.

An easy but effective way to improve your health and quality of life is to make healthy eating a regular part of your life. You are one step closer to being healthier and happy with every healthy meal you eat. You can start your morning breakfast with fruit juice or coconut water, followed by nuts and seeds. This combination can be a meal or snack that wakes you up and makes you feel good.

By consistently choosing healthy meals, you build a foundation for long-term well-being. Over time, these choices can lead to improved physical health, better mental clarity, enhanced emotional stability, and stronger social connections. The journey to a healthier lifestyle begins with simple steps, and eating one healthy meal each day is a manageable and effective starting point. As you continue to prioritize your nutrition, you will likely find that the benefits extend to every aspect of your life, making you feel more vibrant, focused, and content.

Ask yourself

1. When would be my one healthy meal? (Breakfast/Lunch/Dinner)

2. What will be the right meal for me?

3. How it will benefit me in long run?

The key points to remember from this chapter are:

- Well-balanced meals give you energy, keep your mind stable, and fight off sickness.
- Eat breakfast first to calm down and keep your blood sugar level. Fiber and protein will give you energy that lasts.
- Omega-3s, which can be found in fish and nuts, make you smarter and less stressed.
- Simple carbs help you feel good all the time.
- Choose healthy foods that make you feel good and don't limit you for long-term health.
- Eating food with people you care about is good for both your body and your relationships.
- Healthy meals are one simple thing that you can do to improve your health and well-being.

Worksheet: Eat One Healthy Meal

1. When would be my one healthy meal? (Breakfast/Lunch/Dinner)

---

2. What will be the right meal for me?

---

3. How it will benefit me in long run?

CHAPTER 4:
DRINK ENOUGH WATER

Rivers are roads which move, and which carry us whither we desire to go.

- Blaise Pascal

Drinking enough water is crucial for maintaining overall health and well-being. While it may seem like a simple task, many people underestimate the importance of staying adequately hydrated throughout the day. Water is essential for nearly every bodily function, from regulating body temperature to aiding digestion and nutrient absorption.

There are many reasons to drink enough water -

- Water is essential for maintaining the balance of bodily fluids, which are necessary for digestion, absorption, circulation, creation of saliva, transportation of nutrients, and maintenance of body temperature.
- It helps in regulating cell metabolism and biochemical reactions.
- It helps keep joints lubricated and prevents from discomfort and stiffness.
- Water assists in regulating body temperature through sweating and respiration. When you're hot, you sweat, and when that sweat evaporates, it cools your body down.
- Water carries nutrients and oxygen to cells and helps remove waste products from the body through urine and sweat.
- Water is crucial for digestion, as it helps dissolve nutrients and aids in the breakdown of food. It also prevents constipation by softening stools and promoting regular bowel movements.

- Water helps the kidneys remove waste from the blood in the form of urine. Without enough water, waste products can build up and cause various health problems.
- Proper hydration can improve skin health by keeping it moisturized and reducing the risk of dryness, irritation, and premature aging.

So, for the above reasons, one should consume enough water.

How much water is enough?

The amount of water a person needs to consume can vary depending on various factors such as age, sex, weight, climate, physical activity level, and overall health status. However, a general recommendation is to aim for about eight glasses of water a day, which is roughly two litres.

Besides the general recommendation, another method to determine how much water to drink is to pay attention to your body's thirst signals. Drinking when you are thirsty is an excellent strategy to make sure you keep hydrated because thirst is your body's way of telling you that it needs more water. Furthermore, the colour of your urine can also serve as a useful indicator of your level of hydration; clear or pale yellow urine often suggests appropriate hydration, whereas dark yellow urine may indicate dehydration.

It is essential to note that while water is the best choice for hydration, other fluids such as herbal tea, milk, and unsweetened fruit juice can also contribute to overall fluid intake. There are many fruits and vegetables like water melon, musk melon, cucumber etc have high water content and can help maintain hydration levels.

How to consume?

- It is best to sip water regularly.
- Water must not be too cold or too hot.
- Don't drink immediately after having meal.
- Keep a gap of at least 30 minutes after eating.

- Always consume water while sitting.

How to make it a habit?

Making it a habit to consume water regularly can be achieved by incorporating some simple strategies into your daily routine:

- You can set reminders to drink water at regular intervals.
- Carry a water bottle with you.
- You could monitor your consumption by using smart bottles, which are easily available in the market. These bottles not only track your intake but also send reminders to ensure you stay hydrated.

Ask yourself,

1. What is my daily intake of water?

2. How can I include eight glasses of water every day in my daily routine?

3. Have I incorporated water-rich foods like fruits and vegetables into my meals today?

The key points to remember from this chapter are:

- Water helps in maintaining bodily fluid balance, cell metabolism, joint lubrication, temperature regulation, nutrient transport, digestion, waste removal, and skin health.
- General recommendation suggests aiming for about eight glasses or roughly two litres of water per day, but individual needs vary based on factors like age, sex, weight, climate, and activity level.
- Pay attention to thirst cues and urine colour to determine hydration status.
- Water is the best choice for hydration, but other fluids and water-rich foods also contribute to overall hydration.

- Drinking water regularly involves sipping water throughout the day, avoiding extreme temperatures, waiting after meals, and sitting while drinking.
- Establishing a habit of regular water consumption can be facilitated by setting reminders, carrying a water bottle, and using smart bottles to track intake and receive reminders.

Worksheet: Drink Enough Water

1. What is my daily intake of water?

----

2. How can I include eight glasses of water every day in my daily routine?

----

3. Have I incorporated water-rich foods like fruits and vegetables into my meals today?

CHAPTER 5:
WORK ON YOUR HOBBY

"No man is really happy or safe without a hobby"
- William Hosler

Ever feel stressed after work? Do you have a favourite thing to do for fun? That thing, your hobby, is super important! It chills you out, lets you be creative, and makes you feel good about yourself.

In a world where everything happens fast, hobbies teach us to be patient and keep trying. Hobbies let you be creative and express yourself without worrying about rules. Hobbies are great because they help you relax and forget work stress. Whether it's painting, gardening, or playing music, hobbies gives your brain a break, and helps you feel better. When you go back to work, you will feel more energetic and creative.

Doing hobbies isn't just fun; it's really important for leading a good life. Even though work and everyday stuff are busy, spending time on hobbies is super important for feeling happy and growing as a person.

Hobbies also help you meet new friends who like the same things you do. Joining hobby groups lets you hang out with people who share your interests. It's fun and makes you feel like you belong somewhere. With lots of social media apps like YouTube, Instagram, Facebook, and WhatsApp, you can become a social media influencer. You can also build your own group of followers by teaching them something cool. For example, if you like playing a musical instrument, like the guitar, you can teach people how to play it.

You can also make money out of it. Here are some suggestions for you:

- Before you jump in, see if people actually want to buy what your hobby makes. Are there others who like the things you create or the things you know how to do?
- Want to sell the best paintings in town? Take some art classes! This will enhance your hobby stuff even better.
- There are many ways to make money from hobbies. Sell things you make, teach others your hobby skills, or even give advice as a consultant. Choose something you enjoy and that makes sense for your hobby.
- The internet is a giant marketplace. Build a website or use social media to show off your hobby stuff. There are even websites like Etsy where you can sell your crafts!
- Don't try to be a business superstar right away. Sell a few things, see how it goes, and make changes as needed. As your hobby-based business grows, you can do more and more.

Ask yourself,

- What hobbies make me feel most fulfilled?
- What skills have I developed through my hobbies?
- How much time do I want to dedicate to my hobbies each day?

The key points to remember from this chapter are,

- Hobbies connect you with like-minded people, creating a sense of community.

- Social media can amplify this by allowing you to share your passions, teach others, and even build a following.

- Research demand for your creations or skills.

- Improve your skills through classes to enhance your offerings.

- Explore various income avenues, such as selling handmade items, offering lessons, or consulting.

- Utilize online platforms to showcase and sell your work.

- Start small and adapt your approach as you grow.

Worksheet: Work on Your Hobby

1. What hobbies make me feel most fulfilled?

---

2. What skills have I developed through my hobbies?

---

3. How much time do I want to dedicate to my hobbies each day?

CHAPTER 6:
READ AN INSPIRATIONAL QUOTE

"Quotes are like seeds; plant them in your mind, and let them grow."

— Unknown

Reading an inspiring quote can change the way you think and feel about life in a big way. People can feel better, be motivated, and uplifted by inspirational words to go after their dreams, get past problems, and live their best lives.

"*It always seems impossible until it's done*," said Nelson Mandela. This quote emphasizes the idea that problems and tasks often seem too big to handle before we do something about them. It shows how important it is to keep going even when things get hard. When we set our sights on a job or goal, we can achieve things that seemed impossible before. This is a reminder to take on obstacles, because most of the time, you only succeed after getting past your doubts and fears.

Another well-known inspirational quote is by Helen Keller: "*The only thing worse than being blind is having sight but no vision.*" This quote serves as a reminder that having a clear vision for what we want to achieve in life is essential for success. It encourages us to dream big, set goals, and work tirelessly to turn our dreams into reality.

Also, inspirational words can help you feel better and give you hope when things are hard. For example, when things go wrong or facing a tough time, the quote "*When one door of happiness closes, another opens; but often we look so long at the closed door that we do not see the one which has been opened for us*" by Helen Keller, reminds us to stay hopeful and to keep moving forward, even when faced with challenges.

Reading motivational quotes every day helps you to stay focused, inspired, and grateful. Any inspirational quote, whether it's about the power of sticking with something, the importance of being thankful, or the beauty of life's journey, can immediately change our outlook and give us a new sense of purpose and happiness.

I've always been fascinated by quotes. In this book, I have used quotes at the beginning of each chapter. You can easily find quotes in newspapers. I also search on Google and YouTube. Engaging with a quote every day can offer fresh perspectives on self-reflection. Last year, I also made a YouTube channel called *@7Quotesforlife*. I have already put up more than 70 videos. Each video is no longer than 90 seconds.

One of my favourite quote is by Mahatma Gautama Buddha,

"The mind is everything. What you think you become."

This quote motivates me to think about only positive things. The impact of this particular quote is huge, making you believe that you are the creator of your future. You can achieve anything by just thinking about it. That single thought will inspire you to take action every day. Reading a quote each day can really change your life for the better.

In a study conducted in 2005, it was discovered that inspirational quotes effectively enhance confidence, motivation, empowerment, and satisfaction among people dealing with stress, anxiety, depression, mental illness, and substance abuse. In another study published in *Frontiers in Psychology*, in November 2018, researchers found that motivational quotes can boost the self-esteem of patients battling chronic diseases.

Many successful entrepreneurs stay positive and get inspired by successful thoughts and words. Even athletes often chant words or phrases to boost themselves. Inspirational quotes are short but impactful. It takes just few seconds to read. Their messages can stay with you for many years. You probably remembered at least one motivational quote you read long time ago.

From now, assure yourself to read one quote daily. You can also read while travelling to your workplace in the morning.

Ask yourself,

1. Do u feel motivated after reading quotes?

2. Write three quotes that inspire you most.

3. How do the inspirational quotes affect you?

The key points to remember from this chapter are:

- Reading an inspiring quote can change the way you think and feel about life in a big way.
- Motivational and inspiring words encourage people to follow their dreams and get past problems.
- Motivational words have been shown to improve people's self-esteem to overcome their long-term illnesses, which is more proof of their health benefits.
- Many successful entrepreneurs and athletes draw inspiration from quotes to maintain a positive mindset and overcome challenges.

Worksheet: Read an Inspirational Quote

1. Do u feel motivated after reading quotes?

----

2. Write three quotes that inspire you most.?
i--
ii---
iii--

3. How do the inspirational quotes affect you?

CHAPTER 7:
REDUCE SCREEN TIME

"We are all connected to the internet, like neurons in a giant brain."

- Stephen Hawking

In this modern age, where screens seem to be in every part of our lives, cutting down on screen time is becoming increasingly important. Screen types are all around us and take up a lot of our time— whether they're phones, tablets, computers, or TVs.

Have you ever thought of the following,

- How many times we pick our phones?
- How much time we spend on screen?

Now, according to a blog by Josh Howarth,

- Typically, an individual dedicates around 3 hours and 15 minutes to their mobile devices daily,
- While the average number of times they check their phones amounts to 58 times per day.

After reading this blog, I checked my phone to look for the above stats. It was so shocking for me as well. I was spending 4 hours and 45 minutes daily on screens. But it also includes the time when my kids play games and watch YouTube videos on it. The average pick time was also high— 64 times per day. Now it's your turn to check.

However, excessive screen time can have negative effects on both our physical and mental health, making it crucial to find ways to reduce our screen usage.

Physical health

Being in front of screens for long periods of time can cause

- Poor posture
- Eye strain
- Increased risk of obesity and cardiovascular disease.

Mental health

Excessive smartphone screen time has been linked to increased

- Rates of depression,
- Anxiety,
- Stress,
- Constantly staring at screens can also disrupt our sleep patterns, leading to fatigue and irritability.

By reducing screen time, we can encourage more physical activity, promoting better health. We can also give our minds a much-needed break and improve our overall mental health.

Reducing screen time means more time. We can use this time to:

- Read books of your interest.
- Prioritize spending quality time with the people who matter the most and strengthening our relationships.
- Increased productivity and creativity.
- Focus on tasks that matter and pursue hobbies and interests that inspire us.
- Unlock our full potential and achieve greater success in various aspects of our lives.

How to reduce screen time?

Awareness is the key! You might be wondering about the straightforward answer. But it's true and you can be aware by setting a limit on your daily screen time. Now your phone will notify when you have reached the limit. I also applied this strategy. Now while reading this, set your time limit. Initially, it might not be as easy as it seems, because many times you will cross that limit. But you will become aware of your screen time. It will remind you to limit your screen time. However, after making a conscious effort, I managed to reduce it to 2 hours and 30 minutes, which also includes my kids' usage.

There can be many ways to reduce screen time-

- Uninstall all the apps that you haven't used for a long time (at least one month).
- Limit notifications.
- Digital fasting on weekends for three to five hours.
- Allocate specific times during the day for screen usage.

Ask yourself,

1. How much time I spend on screen?

2. How much time I will limit onscreen ?

3. How I will use this saved time?

The key points to remember from this chapter are,

- Negative effects on physical and mental health.
- Physical health issues: poor posture, eye strain, obesity.
- Mental health concerns: depression, anxiety, disrupted sleep.
- Reducing screen time means more time for reading and personal interests.
- Focus on meaningful activities.
- Set daily usage limits.
- Uninstall unused apps.
- Practice digital fasting on weekends (Three to five hours).
- Allocate specific times for screen use.

Worksheet: Reduce Screen Time

1. How much time I spend onscreen?

----

2. How much time I will limit onscreen?

----

3. How I will use this saved time?

CHAPTER 8:
SET A GOAL FOR TODAY

If you want to live a happy life, tie it to a goal not to people or things

-Albert Einstein

What a beautiful quote it is! Isn't it? Having a goal in life provides you with a sense of purpose. And once you reach it, you experience fulfilment. However, this sense of accomplishment isn't something we encounter every day, as we don't achieve such goals on a daily basis.

Set a daily goal

Every day, we have to do many things. We create a to-do list every morning. Some people create a to-do list just before they go to bed, it's a good habit. I have also completed many tasks by creating such lists daily. But, apart from daily routine work, we all have a big goal or dream. You think about this goal but never take action. You know why? This goal feels too big to attain. It seems almost unachievable for now. You can break down your big goal into small, achievable daily goals.

For example, if you want to write a book of 150 pages. You can make it easy by committing to write a half-page every day. In doing so, within a year's time, you'll have completed your book.

So, the next time you craft your to-do list, consider adding the task of writing half a page daily. After one year, you will not be the same person. Now you have achieved your unachievable goal.

How important is feeling of achievement?

The feeling of achievement gives you the motivation to do more. It boosts confidence that now you can do anything. So, it's important to write down your daily goals and complete them to keep alive this feeling of achievement. Setting a goal for today might seem small, but it can make a big difference in how productive and fulfilled you feel. Whether it's finishing a project, learning something new, or simply taking care of yourself, having a goal can give your day direction and purpose.

Ask yourself now,

1. What is your dream or big goal that you want to achieve?

2. How many tasks should I break this significant goal into?

3. When I will achieve this?

The key points to remember from this chapter are,

- Daily tasks are often organized in a to-do list, which is a beneficial habit.
- Large dreams can feel overwhelming; break them into smaller, achievable daily goals.
- To write a 150-page book, commit to writing half a page daily—this leads to completion in a year.
- Set a deadline to complete.

Worksheet: Set a Goal for Today

1. What is your dream or big goal that you want to achieve?

----

2. How many tasks should I break this significant goal into?

----

3. When I will achieve this?

CHAPTER 9:
BE CONSISTENT

"Success isn't always about greatness. It's about consistency. Consistent hard work leads to success. Greatness will come."

– Dwayne Johnson.

In a world obsessed with instant results and quick fixes, consistency is often an overlooked virtue. But the truth is, consistency is the key ingredient to achieving any big or long-term goal. It's the small, regular actions that compound over time to produce remarkable results.

Whether you are aiming to lose weight, learn a new language, or build a successful business, consistency is the bridge that takes you from where you are to where you want to be. It's the unwavering commitment to showing up, day in and day out, even when you don't feel like it.

Michael Phelps: Great example of consistency

When we discuss consistency, athletes often come to mind as prime examples. They maintain their performance levels day in and day out. One such athlete is the most decorated Olympian i.e. Michael Phelps. He shows how being consistent can help you succeed a lot. He trained every day for six years without missing a single session, showing how much he wanted to be the best. Phelps made sure to set clear goals daily and worked hard to get better at swimming. Because of his consistency, he won 23 Olympic gold medals, which is more than anyone else. His story teaches us that if we keep achieving small task every day, we can achieve big things, inspiring people everywhere to chase their dreams with determination.

How to be consistent?

Consistency is easy to maintain but it's very hard at the same time. It's easy when you are serious about it. For example, if you want to have a good physique, then you must remain consistent daily for at least 45 minutes work out. When I say it's hard because we are lazy and procrastinate a lot.

Indeed, consistent action is the bridge between goals and accomplishment. So, how can one develop this essential quality? Here what I follow to maintain consistency.

- Fix a time during day or night. Initially, do it for three days at your fixed time and place.
- Once you have completed 1 cycle of 3 days. Then do it for another 3 days i.e. 2nd cycle.
- Measure your performance and compare it to 1st cycle. It gives you a motivation to go on.
- Take one day rest and then repeat these cycles in the next week.
- Switch off your mobile phone.
- Use time blocking i.e., fix 30 or 40 minutes. It varies from person to person, activity to activity.

What is the best time?

The time before lunch is the most crucial time. Especially between 9:30 to 12 o'clock. During this time, you are more active than any other time of the day. Use this time to maintain consistency for your specific work.

Consistency isn't just being good at something; it's about doing it the same way every time. It means always trying your hardest and never giving up, whether you're at work, with friends, staying healthy, or doing things you love. Consistency helps you reach your goals and make your dreams come true. So, stick with it, and you'll see big changes in your life.

Ask yourself,

1. What task do you aim to maintain consistency in?

2. How much time do you plan to dedicate to this task daily?

3. Over how many cycles do you anticipate its completion?

The key points to remember from this chapter are,

- Consistency is often overlooked but essential for achieving long-term goals.
- It involves steady, regular actions that compound over time to produce remarkable results.
- Athletes like Michael Phelps exemplify the power of consistency in achieving extraordinary success.
- Cultivating consistency requires commitment and discipline.
- Establish a set time and place for your activity, and commit to consecutive cycles of work.
- Monitor progress, draw motivation from improvements, and take necessary rest days.
- Create an environment conducive to consistency by minimizing distractions.
- Utilize time blocking to allocate specific time slots for your task.
- Leverage peak productivity periods, such as the time before lunch, for optimal performance.

Worksheet: Be Consistent

1. What task do you aim to maintain consistency in?

----

2. How much time do you plan to dedicate to this task daily?

----

3. Over how many cycles do you anticipate its completion?

CHAPTER 10:
PLAY A SPORT

"Sport teaches you character, it teaches you to play by the rules, it teaches you to know what it feels like to win and lose."

- Billie Jean King

Playing sports isn't just about staying physically fit; it's also great for keeping your brain healthy, feeling positive, and reducing stress. Let's look at how playing sports can help your mind. Sports make you think fast and plan strategies, which are good for your brain. It also help build connections in your brain, making you smarter and better at solving problems. Plus, when you exercise, your brain releases chemicals that make you feel happy and less worried. The focus and rhythm of sports can also calm your mind and make you feel less stressed.

How important it is?

A few months ago, I found this article titled *"Mental Benefits of Sport."* It was a good article indeed. Being part of a sports team or group can make you feel proud and good about yourself.

- Improves your mood and concentration
- Reduces stress and depression
- Improves sleep habits
- Boost self-confidence

Which sports?

Numerous sports offer rejuvenating effects and require minimal time commitment. Swimming stands out as an excellent sport because it engages all muscle groups during performance. It is also an excellent aerobic exercise that increases your heart rate, improving cardiovascular health. Swimming for 30 minutes daily can give you numerous benefits-

- Strengthens Muscles
- Increases Flexibility
- Weight Management
- Improves Lung Capacity
- Improve Posture

Cycling is a great way to stay healthy and have fun. When you ride a bicycle, you're giving your heart and lungs a good workout, which helps keep them strong. It's also a fantastic way to strengthen your leg muscles and improve your balance and coordination. Cycling can help you

- Manage your weight and reduce the risk of illnesses like heart disease and diabetes.
- Great exercise for people of all ages.
- Help reduce stress and boost your mood.
- And let's not forget, it's a fun way to explore your neighbourhood or enjoy the outdoors.

There are many other sports which you may have already joined. But if you are not playing any of the sport, now you have the option to pick swimming or cycling as your new sport of choice. Both activities can be done alone, without needing a partner or group to accompany you.

My sports routine

I like cycling in the evening with my kids during weekdays. On weekends, I play football with them for 40 minutes. Playing sports is very important for everyone. It makes you stronger, more confident, and less stressful. According to a study, people who participate in sports tend to have higher self-esteem, experience less depression, and enjoy better overall mental and social well-being.

If you are not playing any sport, you are missing out on discovering sports person inside you. START TODAY, AND DO IT EVERYDAY.

Ask yourself,

1. What sport should I engage in?

2. How much time do I intend to dedicate to it?

3. When is the best time for me to play sports?

The key points to remember from this chapter are,

- Sport is for all age groups children, young, and old people.
- It gives you strength and confidence to face challenges in your life.
- Take out at least 30 minutes for cycling or swimming. There can be other sports also.
- Play at least five days.
- Join some nearby sports club.

Worksheet: Play a Sport

1. Which sport should I engage in?

---

2. How much time do I intend to dedicate to it?

---

3. When is the best time for me to play sports?

CHAPTER 11:
SPEND TIME WITH YOURSELF

"Keep taking time for yourself until you are you again."

—Lalah Delia

Time is the most precious, and we get 24 hours every day. We spend it by doing so many tasks throughout the day. We interact with various individuals and exchange ideas. Sometimes we discuss things happening around the world. Sometimes we restrict to our tasks only. Sometimes we feel bored, and sometimes we feel energetic. In an entire day, around 80,000 thoughts courses through our brains, leading to a sense of mental fatigue by evening. Because thoughts travel so fast which takes us from first place to second, second to third and so on? We are either thinking about our past or future. We are not completely present in the present moment. So, it becomes necessary to spend time with ourselves. Spending time with yourself is essential for,

- Personal growth,
- Relaxation
- Self-discovery
- Mindfulness

This is the time when you can just be with your own thoughts and feelings. You don't have to worry about what anyone else thinks. This time alone is called solitude, and it is important for feeling good inside.

Where to pay attention?

In this time, when you are alone and thoughts are flooding your brain. Just switch your attention to yourself and about your work. Now ask yourself, how can I be better what I do? It may be study, job, sports any area of life. So, think about:

- Improvement
- Enhancement
- Polishing your skill
- Positivity around you

It will give you many ideas. Let us do an experiment, consider about enhancing your communication skills. It gives you so many suggestions like,

- Listen to a podcast or watch some video tutorials which gives communication skill lessons.
- Buy a book about techniques to enhance communication skill
- Join some part-time course
- Register yourself for an online course
- Seek help from a friend who has better communication skills
- Practice for 15 to 20 minutes daily

Now, it's time for you to choose the option that suits best with your needs and preferences.

Spending time with yourself gives you many ideas. Spending time is not just about sitting in a quiet place and closing your eyes, but also about doing things that makes you more productive. For example, writing a daily journal, taking a walk, listening to music etc. It can also mean turning off your phone and just enjoying being by yourself. You can also try taking slow breaths or thinking about happy things. It can be 10-20 minutes long. The simplest thing that you can use this time to review your daily routine before you go to bed.

Being alone doesn't have to be lonely. It's a special time for you to relax and be yourself. So, find some time each day to be alone and enjoy the peace and quiet. It's all about doing what makes you happy and calm.

Ask yourself,
1. How much time do you spend with yourself?
2. If yes, write down three positive thoughts that comes to mind.

3. Can you leave rest of the thoughts except above three?

The key points to remember from this chapter are,

- Time is precious, filled with various tasks, interactions, and thoughts throughout the day.
- Constant thoughts can lead to mental fatigue by evening, often making us reflect on the past or future rather than being present.
- Taking time for solitude allows us to connect with our thoughts and feelings without external distractions.
- Engage in activities that bring joy and calm, such as drawing, journaling, walking, or listening to music.
- Being alone can be a special time for relaxation and self-discovery, fostering peace and inner happiness.
- Pay attention to your daily routine for 10- 20 minutes every day.

Worksheet: Spend Time with Yourself

1. How much time do you spend with yourself?

   ----

2. If yes, write down three positive thoughts that comes to mind.

   ----

3. Can you leave rest of the thoughts except above three?

CHAPTER 12:
HAVE ENOUGH SLEEP

"Sleep is the best meditation."

- Dalai Lama

Getting good sleep is really important for staying healthy and feeling your best. Think of sleep like recharging your batteries. Just like your phone needs to be charged to work properly, your body needs sleep to have energy for everything you need to do. When you get enough good sleep, you wake up feeling refreshed and ready to take on the day. You will have more energy to play, work, and concentrate on tasks. Without enough sleep, you might feel tired, forgetful, or cranky.

How much sleep is enough?

The amount of sleep you need can change a lot based on your age, lifestyle, and health. But experts have some general guidelines for most adults. The National Sleep Foundation says that adults aged 18-64 usually need seven to nine hours of sleep each night. Older adults (65 and up) may need a bit less, about seven to eight hours (Hirshkowitz et al., 2015). While everyone is different, getting seven to nine hours is generally good for staying healthy and sharp. A study in *Sleep Health* in 2023 found that not getting enough sleep is linked to higher risks of serious health problems like high blood pressure, diabetes, and mental health issues (Liu et al., 2023). Additionally, a 2024 study in *JAMA Network Open* showed that both too little sleep (less than seven hours) and too much sleep (more than nine hours) can increase the risk of death (Zhou et al., 2024)

How to get a sound sleep?

- Stick to a regular sleep schedule helps your body know when it's time to sleep and wake up. This consistency can make it easier to fall asleep and feel refreshed in the morning.

- Creating a relaxing bedtime routine is also important. Doing calming activities like reading or taking a warm bath before bed can help you unwind and prepare your mind for sleep.
- Your sleep environment matters too. Make sure your bedroom is comfortable—keep it dark, cool, and quiet. If there's noise, try using earplugs or a white noise machine to block it out.
- Avoid screens from phones or TVs at least an hour before bed. The blue light from screens can trick your brain into thinking it's still daytime, making it harder to fall asleep.
- Avoid heavy meals, caffeine, and alcohol before leaving to bed. These can disrupt your sleep.
- You can follow these tips for a better sleep routine and enjoy more restful nights, which will help you feel more energetic and focused during the day.

START TODAY, DO IT EVERYDAY.

Ask yourself,

1. How many hours of sleep do I typically get each night?
2. Do I have a consistent bedtime and wake-up time, even on weekends?
3. What activities do I engage in before bed, and are they relaxing or stimulating?

The key points to remember from this chapter are,

- Getting good sleep is essential for staying healthy and feeling your best, as it acts like recharging your batteries.
- Adults typically need seven to nine hours of sleep each night, with older adults needing slightly less.
- Insufficient sleep can lead to health issues like high blood pressure and diabetes, and both too little and too much sleep can increase the risk of death.
- To improve your sleep, maintain a regular sleep schedule, create a relaxing bedtime routine, and ensure your bedroom is dark, cool, and quiet.
- Avoid screens for at least an hour before bed, and steer clear of heavy meals, caffeine, and alcohol close to bedtime.

Worksheet: Have Enough Sleep

1. How many hours of sleep do I typically get each night?

---

2. Do I have a consistent bedtime and wake-up time, even on weekends?

---

3. What activities do I engage in before bed, and are they relaxing or stimulating?

CHAPTER 13:
VISUALIZATION

"I am enough of the artist to draw freely upon my imagination. Imagination is more important than knowledge. Knowledge is limited. Imagination encircles the world."

-Einstein

Visualization is powerful because it helps us reach our goals by imagining success. When you visualize, you picture in your mind what you want to achieve. This helps your brain get ready as if you were really doing it. It boosts your motivation, focus, and belief in yourself. Athletes use visualization to do better in their sports, imagining themselves winning or performing perfectly. People at work use it too, picturing successful presentations or finishing big projects. When you visualize, you can see what you want clearly, plan how to get there, and feel more confident about reaching your goals. It's a great way to grow and succeed in whatever you set out to do.

Today whatever you are seeing, like laptops, smartphones, buildings, cars etc. are the result of visualization. Everything was visualised before it came into reality. Visualization means a clear mental picture of your dreams, ideas, or goals. It's like drawing a map or a picture of something you want to understand or remember. When you visualize, you are telling your mind that it can become possible and when we visualize something over a long period of time, we start taking action to get that. Visuals have great impact on us. Every day we see numerous examples in various professions.

- Teachers use pictures or diagrams to help students understand difficult concepts. For example, showing a diagram of how plants grow helps students see the process clearly.

- In business, graphs and charts are used to show trends in sales or profits over time. These visuals make it easier for people to understand complex numbers and make decisions based on them.
- Athletes often imagine themselves winning before a competition, which helps them feel more confident and perform better.
- People use visualization to relax or focus during meditation or mindfulness exercises.

In the past, there have been many stories of people using visualization to make the impossible possible.

Natan Sharansky

Natan Sharansky's victory over Garry Kasparov in a 1986 chess match shows how powerful visualization can be. Sharansky was in prison and couldn't play chess with physical boards. Instead, he practiced by imagining games in his mind. During the match with Kasparov, Sharansky impressed everyone by visualizing the chessboard in his head. He could think through moves and plan strategies without using actual pieces. Even though he was up against the world champion, Sharansky stayed calm and won the game. This event highlights how visualization can improve thinking and problem-solving skills, even in tough situations.

Michael Phelps

Michael Phelps, the most decorated Olympian of all time, is renowned not only for his physical prowess but also for his use of visualization as a mental training tool. Before competing in the 2008 Beijing Olympics, Phelps worked extensively with his coach, Bob Bowman, on visualization techniques. Phelps would mentally rehearse each race in vivid detail, imagining every stroke and turn with precision. This practice allowed him to build confidence, anticipate challenges, and mentally prepare for different scenarios. In the finals of the 100m butterfly in Beijing, Phelps famously won by just 0.01 seconds, clinching his seventh gold medal of the Games. His ability to stay focused and execute under pressure was attributed in part to his rigorous visualization routines, which helped him visualize success long before diving into the pool. Phelps' story highlights how visualization can be a potent tool in achieving peak performance, enhancing mental toughness, and overcoming obstacles in pursuit of excellence.

Mike Tyson

Mike Tyson, the legendary heavyweight boxer, also utilized visualization as a key part of his training and mental preparation. Before his fights, Tyson would mentally rehearse his movements, strategies, and knockout punches in great detail. He would visualize himself dominating his opponents in the ring, anticipating their moves, and visualizing his own counters and finishing blows. This practice not only helped Tyson sharpen his focus but also enhanced his confidence and psychological readiness. One of the most famous instances of Tyson's visualization paying off was his fight against Michael Spinks in 1988. Tyson entered the ring with a clear mental picture of how the fight would unfold, and he executed his plan flawlessly, knocking out Spinks in just 91 seconds. This victory cemented Tyson's reputation as one of the most fearsome and dominant boxers of his era. Tyson's story underscores the importance of mental preparation in sports, showing how visualization can translate into decisive victories and iconic performances in the ring.

You can find many similar stories in the history. Visualization is a powerful tool that makes learning easier, helps us make better decisions, and boosts our confidence by allowing us to see possibilities and solutions more clearly. Now it is your turn to use visualization to achieve big in your life.

How can we visualization every day?

You can visualize your day and completing all the important tasks. Just a minute is enough for you to visualize your goals.

Apart from visualizing your day. You can imagine yourself reaching your goal. Close your eyes and picture what success looks like: maybe it's crossing a finish line, finishing a big project, or being praised for something you have done well. See yourself smiling with happiness, feeling proud and satisfied. Think about the steps you took to get there: the hard work, the challenges you faced, and the help you received from others. When you visualize achieving your goal, it helps you stay motivated and focused. It reminds you why you are working hard and gives you confidence that you can make it happen.

Ask yourself,

1. How can I incorporate visualization into my daily routine to enhance my motivation and focus?
2. What are some specific scenarios in my personal or professional life where visualization could improve my performance or decision-making?
3. How can I make my visualization sessions more effective and engaging?

Write the answers of these question at the end of this chapter in a worksheet.

The key points to remember from this chapter are,

- Visualization helps individuals achieve their goals by creating a mental image of success. By picturing desired outcomes, it prepares the brain to act as if those outcomes are already happening, increasing motivation, focus, and self-belief.
- Athletes use visualization to improve performance, such as imagining winning or perfecting their techniques. Similarly, professionals visualize successful presentations or project completions to boost confidence and effectiveness.
- Visualization is also a tool for relaxation and focus, commonly used in meditation and mindfulness practices to enhance mental clarity and calm.

- Sharansky's ability to visualize chess games while in prison demonstrates how visualization can help in strategic thinking and problem-solving under challenging conditions.
- Phelps use of visualization before races helped him achieve peak performance. His ability to mentally rehearse each race contributed to his success.
- To use visualization effectively, spend a minute visualizing your day and key tasks, or imagine achieving your goals. Picture success in detail, including the emotions and steps involved. This practice helps maintain motivation and confidence.

Worksheet: Visualization

1. How can I incorporate visualization into my daily routine to enhance my motivation and focus?

----

2. What are some specific scenarios in my personal or professional life where visualization could improve my performance or decision-making?

----

3. How can I make my visualization sessions more effective and engaging?

CHAPTER 14:
ENCOURAGE YOURSELF

"Start where you are. Use what you have. Do what you can."
—Arthur Ashe

Encouraging yourself is about giving yourself support and motivation. It is like being your own coach who is guiding and asking you to do it anyhow. It is very much necessary. We encourage ourselves many times but occasionally in specific situations, before

- A presentation whether in office, college, schools etc.
- A project meeting.
- An interview.
- A sports competition

We must encourage ourselves daily in the morning by repeating positive affirmations like,

- I am great.
- I am capable of achieving great things.
- I am strong and confident about today and every day.
- Every day, I am closer to my goal.

There can be many more. It is like training your mind to think positively by repeating such lines. It is to prepare yourself today and every day. This practice helps build resilience, improve self-esteem, and keep you focused on your goals. It can change your thought process forever. You will be more confident and stronger. Your mind, who is always storing every single thought and action, will become more focused. Now it will absorb positive things.

Encourage yourself daily to keep your focus on your daily tasks. Write these affirmations on your working desk, or the first page of your diary.

You can also use them as wallpaper on your desktop, laptop, or mobile screen. Each day, there are moments when you might feel low or demotivated. Make sure to repeat these two phrases at least twice and see the magic. In that moment, you will be energized. Motivating and encouraging yourself daily is your responsibility.

Lesson to learn from the frog

While moving through the forest, a pair of frogs unintentionally slipped into a deep trench. The frogs still above measured the depth and concluded very quickly that they would not be able to get out. They started yelling down to the trapped frogs, telling them there was no chance of escape and to give up.

Even after failing several times, one of the frogs persisted in trying to get away. The depressing cries from above eventually caused one of the captive frogs to give up and give in to hopelessness. However, the second frog persisted in moving ahead and was able to emerge from the pit with great difficulty.

"Did you hear us telling you to give up", the frogs that had been safe questioned the fugitive frog? To clarify, the frog said, "I'm deaf. What you were saying was not audible to me. I believed you were encouraging me to keep trying.

Encourage yourself to take risks and keep trying repeatedly until you achieve your goals. Push yourself to see it through to the end. Successful individuals often engage in positive self-talk, especially in sports. For instance, footballer Cristiano Ronaldo says, "I am the best in my mind." This is not arrogance; it is a form of self-encouragement. By believing in himself, he motivates and drives himself to excel.

How to encourage yourself?

We encourage ourselves when we face challenges. We have immense power within ourselves which activates when a challenging task needs to be completed.

David Goggins

David Goggins is famous for his amazing ability to stay strong and determined. His story shows how self-encouragement and pushing through limits can lead to great success. One of his main techniques for staying motivated is called the "Cookie Jar." This idea means keeping a mental collection of his past successes and achievements. When he encounters a difficult situation, Goggins thinks back to these memories to remind himself that he can overcome challenges. Reflecting on his past wins helps boost his confidence and keeps him motivated to continue.

There are different ways to encourage yourself. The best ways I have found are -

- Listening or reading autobiographies of great personalities
- Reading motivational quote
- Watching documentary of soldier's training like, Navy Seal, Commandos, or Hell Week etc.
- Listening to TED talks.
- Reading your goals loud in the morning, if possible, record it while reading. And listen it every day, whenever you feel discouraged.

I know a friend of my colleague who listen encouraging songs while driving to work in the morning.

These ways work. I have implemented all of them. On top of that, your goals are your best encourager. If you do not have a goal, decide one.

"YOU HAVE SO MUCH ENERGY THAT YOU CAN USE TO DO ANYTHING, JUST ANYTHING. ONLY ONE THING YOU HAVE TO DO IS TO FOCUS IT ON YOUR MOST AMBITIOUS GOAL."

Encouraging Genius: Pauline Einstein's Belief in Her Son

When Albert Einstein was young, his mother, Pauline Koch Einstein, received a letter from his school that had a significant effect on her view of her son's future. The letter, sent by one of Albert's teachers, noted that he was struggling in several subjects and not meeting the school's expectations. Pauline, a devoted mother, was deeply worried about Albert's education and overall well-being. She was always a strong supporter, encouraging him even when faced with difficulties.

Despite the discouraging news, Pauline's belief in her son's abilities remained steadfast. She saw that Albert had a unique way of thinking and learning that didn't necessarily fit with traditional educational methods. Her support and confidence were vital in helping Albert pursue his interests in mathematics and physics.

Pauline's encouragement during these challenging times was crucial. She recognized the value in Albert's curiosity and unconventional approach to learning, even when others did not. This unwavering belief played a key role in his eventual success as a ground breaking scientist and one of history's most renowned physicists.

Ask yourself,

1. What positive affirmations or self-talk can I use to motivate myself every day?
2. What are my recent achievements, and how can I build on them?
3. What specific goals do I want to achieve, and what steps can I take right now to move towards them?

The key points to remember from this chapter are-

- Encouraging yourself is like being your own coach. It's essential for staying motivated, building resilience, and improving self-esteem.
- Start each day by repeating positive affirmations.
- The story of the two frogs demonstrates the power of self-belief. One frog, despite hearing discouraging words from others, kept trying and eventually escaped. The lesson is to persist even when others doubt you and to ignore negativity.
- Cristiano Ronaldo's self-talk ("I am the best in my mind") is an example of self-encouragement that drives excellence.
- David Goggins uses his "Cookie Jar" technique, recalling past successes to fuel motivation in difficult times.

Worksheet: Encourage Yourself

1. What positive affirmations or self-talk can I use to motivate myself every day?

----

2. What are my recent achievements, and how can I build on them?

----

3. What specific goals do I want to achieve, and what steps can I take right now to move towards them?

CHAPTER 15:
RECOGNIZE THE TIME WASTERS

"Someday' is a disease that will take your dreams to the grave with you."

- Timothy Ferriss

Time is the most important thing in life. If you have everything, but you do not have time to enjoy that everything, then everything is useless. Sometimes, we find ourselves spending a lot of time on things that don't really matter. These are called time wasters. They can keep us from doing important tasks and make us feel frustrated. But if we learn to recognize them, we can stop wasting time and focus on what's really important.

Time wasters can be activities, habits, or even people that distract us from our goals and priorities. For example, spending too much time on social media or watching TV can be time wasters because they don't help us get things done.

To recognize time wasters, we need to pay attention to how we spend our time. If an activity doesn't bring you closer to your goals or make you happy, it might be a time waster.

If you find yourself spending hours on something without getting much done, it could be a time waster.

If you finish an activity feeling like you wasted your time, it's probably a time waster.

Some things, like video games or scrolling through social media, can be addictive and make it hard to stop. If you have trouble pulling yourself away, it might be a time waster.

In today's digital age, spending too much time on social media, like Facebook, Instagram, or TikTok, can be a big time waster. It's easy to get sucked into scrolling through posts and videos for hours without realizing it.

While it's okay to relax and watch TV sometimes, spending too much time in front of the screen can be a time waster. Especially if you're watching things that don't really interest you or help you learn something new.

Putting off tasks until the last minute or avoiding them altogether is a common time waster. Procrastination can make you feel stressed and overwhelmed when you finally have to do the thing you have been avoiding for long.

Spending too much time thinking and worrying about things that are out of your control can also be a time waster. It is important to address your concerns, but dwelling on them without taking action won't help.

How can we avoid them?

The very easy thing you can do is to follow the four-step algorithm.

Step 1. List all the possible time wasters along with the time you spent doing that.

Step 2. Arrange them in an increasing order of the time spent.

Step3. Pick the top three time wasters.

Step 4. Write down the possible solutions to avoid them.

It is a very effective way to avoid the time wasters and also make yourself more aware of how you spend your time.

Beside this, Having clear goals can help you stay focused and avoid getting side tracked by time wasters. When you know what you want to achieve, it's easier to prioritize your time. If social media or TV is taking up too much of your time, try setting limits for yourself. You can use apps or built-in features on your devices to help you track and limit your screen time. If you are prone to procrastination, breaking tasks into smaller, more manageable tasks can help. This makes it easier to get started and reduces the likelihood of putting things off.

Being mindful of how you spend your time can help you recognize when you're engaging in time-wasting activities. Take regular breaks to check in with yourself and make sure you're staying on track. Time is precious, and we should spend it on things that matter to us. By recognizing common time wasters and taking steps to avoid them, we can make the most of our time and focus on what's truly important. So, next time you catch yourself getting sucked into a time-wasting activity, remember these tips and redirect your energy towards things that bring you joy and fulfilment.

Ask yourself,

1. What activities do you currently spend the most time on, and how do they contribute to your overall happiness and goals?
2. List three specific activities or habits that you consider to be your biggest time wasters.
3. What are your top three personal or professional goals, and how can you align your time management strategies to support them?

The key points to remember from this chapter are,

- Activities, habits, or people that distract from your goals are considered time wasters.
- Pay attention to activities that don't contribute to happiness or goals.
- If you spend hours without productive outcomes, it's likely a time waster.
- Putting off tasks until the last minute can create stress and become overwhelming.
- Spending too much time worrying about uncontrollable factors is also a time waster.
- List potential time wasters and the time spent on them.
- Arrange the list in order of time spent.
- Identify the top three time wasters.
- Develop possible solutions to minimize or eliminate them.

- Having specific goals helps prioritize time effectively and avoid distractions.
- Set limits on social media and TV to reduce time spent on these platforms.
- Divide larger tasks into smaller, manageable steps to combat procrastination.
- Focus on activities that bring joy and fulfilment, ensuring that time is spent meaningfully.

Worksheet: Recognize the Time Wasters

1. What activities do you currently spend the most time on, and how do they contribute to your overall happiness and goals?

----

2. List three specific activities or habits that you consider to be your biggest time wasters.

----

3. What are your top three personal or professional goals, and how can you align your time management strategies to support them?

CHAPTER 16:
STOP OVERTHINKING

"There are always distractions, if you allow them"

- Tony La Russa

Overthinking is becoming more common in this digital age, which is caused by the constant flow of information and connections. People are constantly being stimulated by social media sites, news feeds, and alerts that never end, which can cause analysis paralysis. People feel more anxious and doubtful of themselves when they compare their lives to famous personalities on social media like YouTube, Instagram etc. This can lead to a never-ending cycle of worry. In a world that never really sleeps, the pressure to react right away and keep up with social media can also trap people in a web of over analysis, making it hard to find peace of mind.

When you think too much about something, often worrying or doubting, it is normal to reflect on things, people, and incidents, but overthinking can lead to stress, confusion, and feeling stuck. The first step to recognise it. Are you thinking about something too much, even when you are doing some important work? And that thought is distracting you again and again. You are not able to concentrate and you are constantly paying attention to that single thought.

How Overthinking Affects You

- Constantly worrying about something can make you feel mentally exhausted.
- The more you think, the harder it can be to make a decision, leading to missed chances.
- Overthinking can make your anxiety worse, causing you to focus on fears.

- Focusing too much on the past or future can stop you from enjoying now.

Identify what makes you overthink. Common triggers include:
- Big choices (like big package jobs, cars, or houses)
- Social situations
- Regrets from the past
- Feeling inferior and fear of what others might think

Overthinking often leads to increased anxiety and worry about potential outcomes. This mental burden can make it hard to concentrate on the present, causing distractions.

Recent research has looked into overthinking and how it affects mental health and decision-making. A study by Keng et al. (2019) found that overthinking is linked to higher levels of anxiety and depression, meaning that people who often dwell on their thoughts are more likely to feel negative emotions. Additionally, McEvoy and Br partner (2020) showed that overthinking can make it hard to make decisions, leading to "analysis paralysis," where someone struggles to choose because they think too much. A 2021 study by Zhang et al. highlighted that mindfulness practices can help reduce overthinking and improve emotional control. These findings suggest that addressing overthinking is important for better mental health and decision-making.

How to stop overthinking?

- Give yourself a specific time to think about a problem. When the time is up, make a decision or let it go.
- Use mindfulness techniques like meditation or deep breathing to help you focus on the present.
- When you start to worry, ask yourself if those thoughts are true or just assumptions.
- Instead of just thinking, take small steps towards your goals. Doing something can help clear your mind.

- Sometimes, too much information can make you overthink. Know when to stop researching.
- Share your thoughts with friends or family. They can help you see things differently.
- Understand that mistakes are part of life. Letting go of the need to be perfect can reduce overthinking.
- When you feel overwhelmed, focus on activities you enjoy—like reading, exercising, or hobbies.

Ask yourself,

1. What specific thought or situation is bothering me right now?
2. Is this worry based on facts or assumptions?
3. What activities can I engage in to help clear my mind right now?

The key points to remember from this chapter are,

- Constant worrying can lead to mental exhaustion.
- It can make decision-making difficult, resulting in missed opportunities.
- Overthinking may worsen anxiety, causing you to fixate on fears.
- Excessive focus on the past or future can prevent you from enjoying the present.

Common Triggers include:

- Major life decisions like: jobs, cars, houses etc.
- Social situations
- Past regrets
- Feelings of inferiority and fear of judgment from others

Worksheet: Stop Overthinking

1. What specific thought or situation is bothering me right now?

---

2. Is this worry based on facts or assumptions?

---

3. What activities can I engage in to help clear my mind right now?

CHAPTER 17: READ BOOKS

"A reader lives a thousand lives before he dies...The man who never reads lives only one."

– George R.R. Martin

Reading books is a great way to learn new things, get creative ideas, and relax. It helps you understand different viewpoints, learn new words, and feel inspired. Whether you like stories or facts, books can teach you a lot and make you think in new ways.

Several interesting points have been published in research about the benefits of reading books.

- People who regularly read books, compared to those who consume other types of content, demonstrated a 20% lower risk of mortality.
- Regular reading not only enhances intelligence but also potentially boosts brainpower. As people age, memory and cognitive functions tend to decline, but reading might help mitigate these effects, promoting sharper minds for longer periods.
- Research indicates that reading can significantly reduce stress, potentially lowering it by up to 68%.
- Reading for 30 minutes reduced blood pressure, heart rate, and psychological distress to the same degree as practicing yoga or enjoying humour.

George Orwell has rightly said that, "The best books are those that tell you what you know already." There are many voracious readers like Bill Gates, Warren Buffet, J K Rowling to name a few.

- Warren Buffet reads 500 pages daily.
- Mark Cuban dedicates three hours for reading each day.

- Bill Gates completes 50 books annually.

They are some of the busiest people, still they find time. What about you? Don't say, "I don't find time." In the first chapter, I suggest you to adjust your sleep and wake up time and to get extra hours. You can utilize this time to read your favourite book.

Books are your best friends that show you the right way. You can make a daily habit of reading something. Here are some ways,

- Fix a time (while travelling, before sleeping, during lunch time)
- Read at least for 10-15 minutes. It will crave for more.
- Read about your interests and dreams. If you want to be good speaker, then read about the great speakers. Read about that one skill, in which you want to improve or excel.
- Read autobiographies of famous personalities.

Ask yourself,

1. Which type of books you like to read?
2. What goals can I set for my reading (e.g., pages per day, books per month)?
3. What have I learned from my recent reading?

The key take points to remember from this chapter are,

- Reading books is a great way to learn, generate creative ideas, and relax.
- Regular reading can lower the risk of mortality by 20%, enhance intelligence and brainpower, and potentially reduce stress by up to 68%. Reading for 30 minutes can reduce blood pressure, heart rate, and psychological distress.
- Famous readers like Bill Gates, Warren Buffet, and JK Rowling are avid readers who dedicate significant time to reading.
- To make reading a daily habit, set aside time during travel, before sleeping, or lunchtime, read for 10-15 minutes, and read about your interests or dreams.
- Reading about famous personalities' autobiographies can also help you improve or excel in certain skills.

Worksheet: Read Books

1. Which type of books you like to read?

----

2. What goals can I set for my reading (e.g., pages per day, books per month)?

----

3. What have I learned from my recent reading?

CHAPTER 18:
WRITE SOMETHING

"Start writing, no matter what. The water does not flow until the faucet is turned on."

- Louis L'Amour

We all have a voice inside us encouraging us to write a novel, start a blog, or write a meaningful letter. But with emails, texts, and endless digital content, finding time for daily writing can seem like a rare treat. However, writing regularly has benefits beyond creating content for others to read. It can actually help improve your personality, making you more focused and confident.

Writing every day can make you feel happier and less stressed. Even if you just write a little bit each day, it can have a big impact on your life. Writing helps you express how you feel. Whether you're happy, sad, or angry, writing down your thoughts can make you feel better. It's like talking to a friend who listens without judgment.

In 2013, an experiment was conducted to investigate the impact of expressive writing in New Zealand. A group of 49 people were asked to write about their life events or their daily routines. It was discovered that individuals who spent 20 minutes each day on expressive writing for three consecutive days following a medically necessary biopsy healed faster compared to a control group.

Daily writing has many benefits:

- When you write, you focus on what's happening in the moment, which can calm your mind and make you feel more peaceful.
- Writing lets you think about yourself and what you want in life. It's like having a conversation with yourself. You can think about your dreams, goals, and the things that make you happy.

- Writing makes you more creative. You can write stories, poems, or anything else you can think of. Being creative can make you feel happy and excited.
- Writing can help you solve problems in your life. When you write about your problems, you see them more clearly and come up with solutions. It's like having a plan to make things better.
- Writing can improve how you talk to other people. When you write every day, you get better at expressing yourself. You can communicate your ideas and feelings more clearly to others.

A 2019 study showed that a six-week writing program can help people who have experienced trauma in the past year by increasing their resilience and lowering symptoms of depression, stress, and overthinking. 35% of those people who began the program with signs of clinical depression no longer showed these symptoms by the end of the session.

If you are not a regular writer. You can start writing about your daily routine in one paragraph. It will help you to make yourself better every day in many things. Because writing will make you more attentive about your daily things. You will be more aware about your actions. You can start writing by

- Keeping a journal/diary
- Fixing 10 – 20 minutes every day
- Using some writing tool or apps

Apart from these, you can start a blog to write about your hobby. For example, if you like to talk about cricket. Then you can start writing about cricket on your blog. There are so many things and themes that you can select. It can be music, sports, educational content, dance, art, cultural etc.

You can set a goal of writing at least four lines every day. It is an achievable goal. You can also start to write down the thoughts or ideas that arise to you every day.

I like inspirational stories, so I read and write about them.

So, grab a pen and paper or open a blank document on your computer, and start writing. You will be surprised at how much better you feel. When you start writing, many ideas and thoughts arise in your mind.

Ask yourself,

1. What voice inside you encourages you to start writing, and what specific writing project are you considering (e.g., a novel, blog, letter)?
2. How does writing regularly affect your personality and overall well-being?
3. How can setting aside 10 or 20 minutes each day for writing make a difference in your life?

The key points to remember from this chapter are,

- Regular writing enhances focus, confidence, and creativity.
- Writing helps in clarifying problems and brainstorming solutions.
- Allocate 10-20 minutes each day for writing to reap its benefits.
- Keep a journal, start a blog, or use digital tools to maintain a writing habit.
- Write about personal interests or daily experiences to stay engaged and motivated.
- Studies show that expressive writing can accelerate healing after medical procedures and reduce symptoms of depression and stress.

Worksheet: Write Something

1. What voice inside you encourages you to start writing, and what specific writing project are you considering (e.g., a novel, blog, letter)?

----

2. How does writing regularly affect your personality and overall well-being?

----

3. How can setting aside 10 or 20 minutes each day for writing make a difference in your life?

CHAPTER 19: WATCH YOUR THOUGHTS

"Watch your thoughts, for they will become actions. Watch your actions, for they will become... habits. Watch your habits for they will forge your character. Watch your character, for it will make your destiny."

— Margaret Thatcher

Have you ever felt like your mind is a busy place, filled with lots of thoughts running around? Well, there is a simple way to feel peaceful inside, even when things feel chaotic. It's all about watching your thoughts like you are watching yourself in the mirror.

You continuously collect information through your five senses, which act as input devices for your brain. Your brain then processes this information similarly to a computer system. For example, if you focus on a movie, your brain will mainly process information related to it. Any details you have about the movie will be reviewed and analysed by your mind.

Experiment with your brain by carrying your attention to something. It can be about an event, a person, or sports etc. Whatever you think, it will appear in your brain immediately. This is the related information about that event, person or sports etc. These small thread of information is known as thoughts. Every single thought carries enormous information. When you watch these thoughts without getting caught up in them, you start to feel peaceful inside. It's like finding a quiet space inside yourself, even when things around you are noisy or busy. This peace comes from knowing that your thoughts don't control you.

Sometimes, our thoughts can be like worries that keep bothering us. But when you watch them from a distance, they don't seem as scary or important. You realize that worrying doesn't help, and you can let go of those thoughts more easily.

Now, the decision is yours to watch or to be busy with them. Lord Buddha says "Thoughts can lead to suffering if they are driven by ignorance, attachment, or aversion. By becoming aware of the nature of our thoughts, we can break free from this cycle."

Of course it's not easy to break the cycle. That's why you have to just watch them. And watch it every day. Just two minutes is enough to start with. It looks very easy to watch thoughts without taking any action on them. But it's not.

Watching your thoughts helps you feel more peaceful and comfortable. When your mind is calm and peaceful, you start to notice the little things that bring you joy, like the sound of birds chirping or the warmth of the sun on your face. You become more grateful for the present moment and find happiness in simple things.

It is very important in today's life, when everyone is so busy just running all the time from home to their workplace, college, or office. Once you start sitting with yourself, you will feel like life has changed. Your attitude towards things and situation will change. Your thoughts are so powerful than you ever imagined.

"Every thought that we think is creating our future" -Louise Hay

Power of your thought

One day, a yogi and his disciple arrived in a big city with no money, needing food and shelter. The disciple suggested they sleep in a park, but the yogi proposed they stay in a hotel instead. The disciple was incredulous, but the yogi explained that intense focus could manifest their desires. The yogi meditated deeply and, after ten minutes, led the disciple to a hotel where the manager, sensing their predicament, offered them food and lodging in exchange for work. Surprised, the disciple asked how this was possible, and the yogi revealed that powerful thoughts, when concentrated and believed in strongly, can materialize into reality. He explained that concentration, detailed visualization, and unwavering faith in one's thoughts are crucial for this process. The disciple realized he needed to improve his concentration and visualization skills to harness this power effectively, and the yogi confirmed that mastering these abilities would enable him to use the power of thoughts successfully.

Watching your thoughts also means being kind to yourself when negative thoughts pop up. Instead of judging yourself harshly, you can acknowledge those thoughts and let them go with kindness and compassion.

It is a simple practice that can bring a lot of peace and calmness into your life. By treating your thoughts like passing clouds, you can find a quiet space within yourself and appreciate the present moment more fully. So, next time your mind feels busy, take a moment to watch your thoughts and feel the peace within.

A few years back, I was afraid to deliver a presentation on big stages where there was a huge audience. Many times, I got nervous while delivering my presentation. But since then, I focused on my stage fear. Many questions following the answers came in my mind. Where does it come from? And why does it happens? I found that the lack of connection between me and the audience is the key issue. So, I started to ask them their name and what they know about the topic before I actually start my presentation. In that way, by watching closely my thoughts about stage fear. I got the solution. So, you can too!

It is very important and necessary to know about our thoughts. What we think and how we think? When I say what I think means about a person, place or events. When I say about how we think means in positive or negative way. So, it is very important to watch and become aware of our thoughts.

Story about a Monk

A monk, who has not yet achieved enlightenment, is sent by Gautam Buddha to share his teachings. Buddha tells him that while he may not be able to deeply impact others, he should use the opportunity for his own growth. Buddha advises the monk to stay watchful and calm, even if people react with anger, refuse to help him, or he faced hardships like hunger. What's important is not how many people he influences, but how well he maintains his own awareness and composure. Buddha will be pleased if the monk returns having learned to observe and control his own reactions.

Ask yourself,

1. How does my mind feel right now? Is it busy or calm?

2. Do I tend to focus more on positive or negative thoughts?

3. What steps can I take to watch my thoughts for just two minutes every day?

The key points to remember from this chapter are,

- Feelings of a busy mind can be managed by observing thoughts without getting caught up in them, similar to watching clouds in the sky.
- The brain collects and processes information from the senses, much like a computer, focusing on whatever you direct your attention towards.
- Directing your focus to different subjects creates related thoughts. Observing these thoughts without attachment helps one achieve inner peace.
- Viewing worries from a distance reduces their impact and helps in letting go of them more easily.
- Buddha emphasizes the importance of watchfulness over the content of thoughts. By being aware of thoughts without acting on them, one can avoid suffering caused by ignorance, attachment, or aversion.
- Regularly practicing thought observation, even for just two minutes a day, helps in maintaining calmness and noticing simple joys in life.

Worksheet: Watch Your Thoughts

1. How does my mind feel right now? Is it busy or calm?

----

2. Do I tend to focus more on positive or negative thoughts?

----

3. What steps can I take to watch my thoughts for just two minutes every day?

CHAPTER 20:
FOCUSED TOWARD YOUR GOALS

What you focus on grows

-Esther Hicks

Having goals in life keeps us motivated. Without having a goal, you are like a game with no target. Imagine a football game without goalposts or cricket without stumps and boundary lines. Goals make you a stronger person. Bigger the goal, the greater you are. Focusing on your goal can make a big difference in your life. Maybe it's something you have always wanted, like becoming a doctor or traveling the world. Once you know your dream, you are ready to begin the journey toward making it real.

Focusing on your big dream helps you see things more clearly. It's like having a flashlight in the dark—it shows you where to go. When you know what you want, it's easier to make choices and do things that help you get there.

Achieving your big dream doesn't happen all at once. It's like climbing a ladder—one step at a time. Each little step you take gets you closer to your goal. Even if progress seems slow, every small step counts.

Going after your big dream teaches you a lot along the way. You learn new things, like how to overcome challenges and how strong you really are. Even if you fail sometimes, you grow from the experience and become better.

When people see you going after your big dream, it inspires them to chase their own dreams too. Your determination and hard work shows them that anything is possible if you believe in yourself. You become a role model for others to follow.

Every time you get closer to your big dream, it's worth celebrating. Whether it's a small achievement or a big milestone, taking time to pat yourself on the back keeps you motivated. It reminds you of how far you've come and encourages you to keep going. Chasing and focusing on your big dream is not always easy. There are bumps in the road and obstacles to overcome. But when you focus on your ultimate goal, it gives you the strength to keep going, no matter what. You learn to be tough and resilient.

Ten years ago, I read this story in a newspaper which was about a king and the painting of the hen. It demonstrates the power of focus and determination towards your goal.

The King and painting of the Hen

Once, a king asked his artists to paint a picture of a hen, but he wanted more than just a visual representation. He desired a painting that captured the true essence of the hen. The artists worked diligently and created several beautiful paintings. Although the king liked some of them, he found it hard to choose the best one.

One of his ministers suggested a test: since hens have a tendency to peck at things, if a painting were truly realistic, the hens should peck at it. The king agreed and had a group of hens brought in to see each painting. To everyone's surprise, none of the hens pecked at the paintings. Frustrated, the king ordered the minister to create a painting so lifelike that every hen would peck at it. If he failed, the minister would face life imprisonment. The minister asked for six months to complete the task, and the king granted his request.

After six months, the minister returned, but he had no painting with him. Instead, he set up his easel and began to paint on the spot. When the painting was finished and the hens were brought in, every hen pecked at the painting, just as the minister had predicted. The king was curious about the minister's methods, asked why it took him six months to create a painting he could have finished in a day. The minister explained that he spent the entire time living with the hens, carefully observing their behaviours and understanding their true nature.

The story demonstrates that true awareness and understanding come from deeply engaging with and observing what you are studying, rather than just scratching the surface. This highlights the power of focus and thorough observation.

Focusing can be challenging, with so many distractions we face today. But you can improve your focus by being more aware about the things you do. Here are some strategies that can help you focus:

- Break down what you need to achieve into specific, manageable tasks.
- Identify the most important task
- Turn off your distractions like your phone or social media
- Allocate time blocks (15-25 mins) for that task
- Do at least three to four time blocks, taking a five-minute break

Now, there are some questions that might have been raised in your mind like, why 15-25 minutes of time blocks in one go, while I can sit for hours doing that task. Because we are not specific in those hours.

Focusing on a single task for an extended period can be more challenging than it appears. Our brains have accumulated a vast amount of information over the years, and this information is interconnected. The brain is a powerful processor, capable of quickly shifting from one task to another. To improve focus, it's essential to practice the suggested routine daily.

According to a study published in the *European Journal of Social Psychology* in 2010, it takes approximately 10 weeks or 66 days for a new behaviour to become a natural part of your daily routine.

There are many other factors that we need to pay attention to

- Avoid multitasking
- Create a task list
- Practice relaxation techniques like meditation, deep breathing

- Establish a routine at least during working days

Ask yourself,

1. What is the most important task I need to focus on right now?
2. How long can I realistically focus on a task before needing a break?
3. What lessons can I learn from the story of the king and the painting of the hen about understanding and focus?

The key points to remember from this chapter are,

- Achieving your goals takes time and effort, similar to climbing a ladder—every small step counts.
- Pursuing goals teaches resilience and self-discovery, helping you grow from failures and obstacles.
- The story of the king and the hen illustrates that deep observation and understanding are crucial for achieving your goals.
- True mastery comes from immersing yourself in your subject, not just superficial understanding.
- Break down goals into manageable tasks and prioritize them.
- Limit distractions by turning off notifications and creating a focused work environment.
- Use focused work periods (15-25 minutes) followed by short breaks to maintain concentration.

Worksheet: Focused Toward your Goal

1. What is the most important task I need to focus on right now?

----

2. How long can I realistically focus on a task before needing a break?

----

3. What lessons can I learn from the story of the king and the painting of the hen about understanding and focus?

CHAPTER 21: POSITIVE ATTITUDE

"Keep your face always toward the sunshine and shadows will fall behind you."

— Walt Whitman

From the moment we wake up, we start making decisions. The alarm rings, and we find ourselves tossing and turning in bed, debating whether to get up right away or hit snooze for another 15-20 minutes, as we often do. Then we decide whether to exercise outside or inside and what to wear for the day. Every choice, big or small, has both positive and negative aspects. Ultimately, it's up to you to decide how you perceive these choices and the approach you take towards them. The decisions you make shape your attitude and, ultimately, define your life.

Having a positive attitude can make a huge difference in your life. It's not just about seeing the bright or positive side of things but also about how you deal with problems and interact with others.

Positive attitude

- Is a mindset that focuses on the good aspects of any situation.
- Expecting favourable outcomes and to believing that things can get better.
- Approaching challenges with optimism. It involves looking for solutions rather than dwelling on problems.
- Maintaining hope even in difficult times, and seeing opportunities in setbacks.

Wilma Rudolph: A Story Positive Attitude

Wilma Rudolph's story is a remarkable testament to the power of a positive attitude and perseverance. Born on June 23, 1940, in Clarksville, Tennessee, she was the 20th of 22 children in a family struggling financially. As a child, Wilma faced severe health challenges, including polio, which left her with a weakened left leg. Doctors feared she might never walk normally again.

Despite these obstacles, Wilma maintained an unshakable positive attitude. With her mother's encouragement, she embarked on a rigorous physical therapy regimen, determined to overcome her physical limitations.

Wilma's hard work and optimism continued to drive her success at Tennessee State University, where she trained under coach Ed Temple. Her efforts culminated at the 1960 Rome Olympics, where she achieved historic triumphs. Competing in the 100 meters, 200 meters, and 4x100 meter relay, Wilma won three gold medals, becoming the fastest woman in the world and earning the nickname "The Tornado."

Wilma Rudolph's achievements extended beyond her athletic prowess. She used her platform to advocate for sports and education, emphasizing the importance of a positive mindset and hard work.

What does it mean to have a Positive attitude?

A positive mind handles stress better and bounce back from setbacks easily. You feel better about yourself and believe in your abilities. It also affects your health. People with a positive attitude have healthier blood pressure, lower risk of heart problems, strong immune system, and live longer.

A positive attitude can improve your relationships with others. People having positive attitude are better listeners and more empathetic, which helps in understanding others and resolving conflicts. When you are positive, you are more likely to attract supportive and like-minded friends. Positivity helps you resolve disagreements more constructively.

Positive people are often more motivated and enthusiastic about their work, leading to better performance. Positivity helps in creating a supportive team environment. It encourages collaboration and mutual support. When facing work challenges, positive thinkers are better at finding creative solutions and staying motivated.

How to Develop a Positive Attitude?

It is not easy to be positive all the time. But it's not impossible either. It's a habit that you have to cultivate by implementing it every day. By practicing it every day in small things, you can build positive attitude. Take time each day to think about the things you're grateful for. Keeping a journal where you write down positive things about yourself. It will help to shift your focus to what's good in your life.

When you catch yourself thinking negatively, try to reframe it. For example, if you're frustrated about a mistake, think about what you can learn from it rather than focusing on the failure.

Spend time with positive people who lift you up. Avoid those who drag you down and engage in activities that make you feel good.

Positive self-talk

It is very important to pay attention to your self-talk. Whatever you're talking to yourself every moment or day, your mind is always continuously recording you. So be careful what you tell yourself every day. Because repetition has immense power. Talk to yourself in a positive way. Instead of criticizing yourself, use encouraging words and affirmations to boost your confidence.

Set small, realistic goals and celebrate your achievements. This helps you stay motivated and reinforces your positive attitude. Mindfulness and meditation can help you stay calm and focused. Spend a few minutes each day being aware of your thoughts and feelings. When faced with a problem, concentrate on finding solutions rather than dwelling on the issue. This approach helps you stay proactive and positive.

Overcoming Challenges to Staying Positive

Everything has two sides whether it's a coin or, a situation— positive and negative. It's not always easy to stay positive. So, we face challenges like self-doubt, stressful situations, negative environments. But we have to practice positivity. So that it becomes a habit. We must learn from the sportspeople. Some times they lose games, sometimes they win, but they never leave practicing. They continuously improve every day.

Ask yourself,

1. What decisions do I make every morning, and how do they shape my day?

2. What small daily habits can I implement to cultivate a more positive attitude?

3. What small, realistic goals can I set for myself this week?

The key points to remember from this chapter are,

- Every decision we make, starting from the moment we wake up, shapes our attitude and defines our lives.
- Embracing a positive attitude—one that focuses on solutions, maintains hope, and learns from challenges—can significantly enhance our well-being, relationships, and overall success.
- Positivity is a skill that can be developed through daily practices, such as gratitude, positive self-talk, and mindful reflection.
- By cultivating this mindset, we can navigate life's challenges more effectively and inspire others to pursue their own dreams.

Worksheet: Positive Attitude

1. What decisions do I make every morning, and how do they shape my day?

----

2. What small daily habits can I implement to cultivate a more positive attitude?

----

3. What small, realistic goals can I set for myself this week?

CHAPTER 22:
CHALLENGE YOURSELF

Challenge yourself ; it's the only path which leads to growth

- Morgan Freeman

We all go on vacations. What you think— when you are more excited to visit same place that you have already visited or to visit a new place. OK, let me tell you and everybody knows, its VISITING A NEW PLACE. There are many situations in life. We are excited to

- Play new games.
- Put on a new dress.
- Try new skill
- Drive a new vehicle

So basically, we are excited about new things because it gives us a sense of experiencing something different.

Now think again for a moment, what did it feel like driving a new vehicle, let's say a car or bike. It was a challenge for us at first to learn about the features. How it operates? But the second time when we drive, it was not as challenging as it was before. And after some time, we do not care much about it.

We feel safe when we stick to what we already know. But you grow when you take challenges, when you want to step outside your comfort zone. When you learn new thing and experience a different environment.

Life is like an exciting adventure full of opportunities to learn and grow. One of the best parts of this adventure is when we challenge ourselves to do things that might seem a bit scary at first. But it's important to take on challenges because they

- Help us to grow,
- Help us to learn
- Help us to gain a self confidence
- Build a positive attitude
- Build a winner mind set.

When we challenge ourselves, we are setting goals that seem unachievable but also exciting. These goals push us to work harder and be our best selves. Challenges can be tough, but they also help us become stronger and more resilient. Resilience is like a superpower that helps us bounce back from difficult times. When we face challenges, we learn that we are capable of handling whatever life throws our way.

Sometimes, things don't go the way we planned, and we might face setbacks or failures along the way. But instead of seeing failure as the end of the road, we can see it as a chance to learn and grow. Every mistake teaches us something valuable and helps us get closer to success.

Throughout history, there are many stories of people who never gave up despite facing challenges.

Sylvester Stallone

Born with a facial injury that affected his speech, he faced tough times growing up. Despite struggling as an actor with little money, he never gave up on his dream. His script for "Rocky," inspired by a real-life boxer, was rejected by many studios before finally getting made. But Stallone refused to let anyone else play the lead role. The movie became a huge hit, turning him into a major star.

Serena Williams

Serena Williams is a remarkable tennis player who has faced many challenges throughout her career. She has dealt with tough losses in Grand Slam tournaments and personal health problems, yet her ability to bounce back is truly impressive. Despite these obstacles, she has repeatedly found a way to overcome them and reclaim her spot as one of the best in the sport. Her journey is not just about winning matches but also about demonstrating extraordinary strength and persistence. Serena's story highlights the power of determination and the human spirit's capacity to rise above difficulties and continue striving for greatness.

Daily challenges

You can face daily challenges by setting short-term goals. For example, commit to writing five lines on any topic every day or dedicate time to learn a new skill. Keep a journal to track your daily progress. There will be times when you are busy with other tasks and struggle to find time for your planned activities. Overcoming these moments becomes your challenge. Your goal is to ensure that you complete today's tasks, no matter what.

You can include several small challenges in your daily routine that will pay off over time. It can be anything in any domain, like improving personal challenge, physical challenge, social challenge etc. Some of the challenges that you can take are:

- Wake up earlier than you usually do.
- Take longer walks than you normally would.
- Use your phone only when necessary.
- Speak up only when it's needed.
- Take two off-screen breaks of 20 minutes each throughout the day.

The above challenges are not limited. You can add many more as per your schedule and requirement. But these are some general challenges that we must take. They will make you more aware and attentive in your daily chores. Once you complete any of the given challenges for four to five days in row. It will give you feel of achievement. You will want to continue that challenge for longer period of time and finally it become a habit. That habit to complete a specific challenge at a particular time will make you better every day.

You can take support from your friends and family members if you find it difficult to complete a challenge. You can ask for advice from an expert. Collaborate with others doing the similar work.

Ask yourself,

1. What are some small daily challenges you could set for yourself to build new habits?
2. Think of a skill or activity you've always wanted to try. What steps can you take to start learning or practicing it?
3. What lessons can you learn from Sylvester Stallone's story about persistence and success? How can you apply these lessons to your own life?

Write the answers in the provided worksheet at the end of this chapter.

The key points to remember from this chapter are,

- Facing new challenges helps us grow, learn, and develop self-confidence. It's through these experiences that we build a positive attitude and a winning mindset.
- Historical figures like Sylvester Stallone and Serena Williams demonstrate how persistence and determination in the face of challenges can lead to extraordinary success.
- Don't hesitate to seek support from friends, family, or experts if you find it challenging to meet your goals. Collaborating with others can also be beneficial.

Work Sheet: Challenge Yourself

1. What are some small daily challenges you could set for yourself to build new habits?

---

2. Think of a skill or activity you have always wanted to try. What steps can you take to start learning or practicing it?

---

3. What lessons can you learn from Sylvester Stallone's story about persistence and success? How can you apply these lessons to your own life?

CHAPTER 23:
TAKE IMMEDIATE ACTION

"Action is the foundational key to all success."

— Pablo Picasso

We have all heard the phrase, "Don't put off until tomorrow what you can do today," but why is it so important to act immediately?

You have seen that the majority of people thinking to start something but not taking action. They are discussing the ideas with their friends, family everywhere but not taking a step. If this idea is worthwhile and you believe wholeheartedly, you must start executing it.

Opportunities do not always last forever. For instance, if you spot a job of your interest or a new chance you want to pursue, acting quickly can be crucial. Delaying might mean you'll miss out. Remember the Chinese proverb "The best time to plant a tree was 20 years ago. The second-best time is now." Essentially, if you have not started yet, now is the time to act!

I often ask students what they want to do or what do they want to become? How they look about future. I ask them to know their objective. They all have the idea. But only few acting and taking serious action on it.

For example, if you want to become a software developer, be one. What's stopping you? Join a course, search about it, watch videos related to it, search for tutorials, or ask from experts. There are various options available to choose from, it is easy and you can find many ways. But you have to try searching, you have to go out to enquire about courses. It's you who have to take the first step. Procrastination stops you take immediate action.

Suppose you want to be expert at playing the guitar, so go and buy a guitar first. Now you have bought then you will have to learn how to play. It's like compelling yourself to do this work. Make it necessary for you.

When I bought my first car, I did not know how to drive a car. But now because I have to drive, I learned with the help of my brother.

Stick the cup on your own and then you will be forced to complete the task.

There are some interesting study by researchers and psychologist related to procrastination:

- In a recent study of 323 undergraduate students, approximately 81% were identified as procrastinators, while only 19% were not regular procrastinators.
- The average person spends 218 minutes per day, or about 55 days each year, avoiding essential tasks.

So how can you take immediate action. It is a habit of not delaying. Everything we do regularly becomes a habit. So by practicing anti-delaying tactics, we can develop this habit. Here are some easy ways that you can follow:

- Create an environment to forced yourself to work
- Dedicate a fixed time
- Set a reminder to do a particular task
- Set a deadline and achieve that anyhow

Taking immediate action leads you to take more and more steps, and eventually, you will find yourself completing the work.

Ask yourself,

1. What are some small daily challenges you could set for yourself to build new habits?
2. Think of a skill or activity you've always wanted to try. What steps can you take to start learning or practicing it?

3. What lessons can you learn from Sylvester Stallone's story about persistence and success? How can you apply these lessons to your own life?

Write the answers in the worksheet provided at the end of this chapter.

The key points to remember from this chapter are,

- People generally feel more excited about visiting new places or trying new things rather than sticking to familiar routines.
- Facing new challenges helps us grow, learn, and develop self-confidence. It's through these experiences that we build a positive attitude and a winning mindset.
- Historical figures like Sylvester Stallone and Serena Williams demonstrate how persistence and determination in the face of challenges can lead to extraordinary success.
- Setting and tackling small, daily challenges can lead to personal growth and positive habits. Examples include waking up earlier, taking longer walks, or limiting phone use.
- Don't hesitate to seek support from friends, family, or experts if you find it challenging to meet your goals. Collaborating with others can also be beneficial.

Worksheet: Take Immediate Action

1. What are some small daily challenges you could set for yourself to build new habits?

----

2. Think of a skill or activity you've always wanted to try. What steps can you take to start learning or practicing it?

----

3. What lessons can you learn from Sylvester Stallone's story about persistence and success? How can you apply these lessons to your own life?

CHAPTER 24:
LISTEN MUSIC

"Music is what tells us that the human race is greater than we realize."

— Napoleon Bonaparte

Music, in all its forms, makes everything more beautiful and plants a seed in the heart. It has the power to enhance our experiences, touch our emotions, and create lasting impressions. Music plays an important role in boosting one's emotions. Since childhood, we have experienced music during school and college days. Music has had a strong relation with humans from ancient times. We have seen different types of instruments and music forms.

Music acts as a powerful catalyst by influencing our feelings, sparking creativity, and driving social change. It helps people express and understand their emotions, while also inspiring new ideas for artists and writers. Music has been used in social movements to bring people together and highlight important issues. In therapy, it can help with healing, reduce stress, and improve mental functions. Additionally, music connects people from different cultures, helping them understand each other through a shared love of rhythm and melody.

Listening to music every day is more than just a pleasant pastime. It's a practice with numerous benefits for our well-being. Whether it's classical, jazz, pop, or any other genre, daily exposure to music can enhance various aspects of our lives.

- Music triggers the release of dopamine, a neurotransmitter associated with pleasure and reward.
- It can help alleviate feelings of stress and anxiety, making music a natural and enjoyable way to manage daily pressures.

- Music has been found to positively influence cognitive functions such as memory and attention.
- Music during workouts serves as a distraction from fatigue, making physical activity more engaging and less monotonous.

Research has shown that calming music can lower cortisol levels, the hormone related to stress, and promote relaxation.

What a beautiful quote by Alan Watts-

"When we listen to music, we are not listening to the past, we are not listening to the future; we are listening to an expanded present."

"Being in present", as we have heard from the religious gurus, saints, from our elders, and have read from books to be aware about the present and that's the best way to live a life.

According to intriguing research from Johns Hopkins, keeping your brain active as you age can be effectively achieved by listening to or playing music. This activity offers a comprehensive mental exercise.

Generally, we play music as we are feeling at that moment and get lost in an imaginary world. If that moment is about a bad situation and we feel sad, we must not play sad music because, it works as a catalyst in such moments. Instead, if you really want to play some music, tune into some cheerful and motivational songs.

Although finding a dedicated time for music is difficult. But you can find it when commuting to your work place in the morning. Listening motivational songs in the morning can make you more productive.

Ask yourself,

1. How can I incorporate more music into my daily routine?
2. Have I ever used music as a tool for relaxation or stress relief?
3. How can I use music to create a more positive environment in my life?

The key points to remember from this chapter are,

- Music enriches our experiences and enhances emotions.
- Listening to music daily offers many benefits, including the release of happy hormones, reduced stress and anxiety, and improved cognitive functions.
- Listening to uplifting music can boost productivity and positivity, making it essential to choose music that aligns with our current mood.
- Music invites us to be present, providing a mental exercise that can enhance our overall quality of life.

Worksheet: Listen Music

1. How can I incorporate more music into my daily routine?

----

2. Have I ever used music as a tool for relaxation or stress relief?

----

3. How can I use music to create a more positive environment in my life?

CHAPTER 25:
WORK ON YOUR SKILL

"Continuous improvement is better than delayed perfection."

— Mark Twain

Consider a skill that, with just a small daily improvement, could elevate your performance in your job. Focus on enhancing that skill each day. If you are unsure which skill to focus on, take a moment to identify one that you regularly use in your daily routine—whether it's typing, painting, singing, playing an instrument, or a sport. Aim to improve that skill just a little each day, striving to be better than you were yesterday.

For example, if your job is that of a data entry operator, then you already know that what matters in this job.... yes, you are right, SPEED. If you work on Excel and you are not as fast as you should be, then it will take much time to work on it. So, you can find out one short key combination every day and practice it as a part of your routine. Use it every time whenever it's required throughout the day. Now think, how you will be in using Excel after a month, six months, or a year. Yeah, it's right that you just thought of— an EXPERT!

Skill development usually happens through steady, small improvements rather than big leaps. Practicing a little every day helps you get better over time. Originating from Japan, Kaizen is a very famous and well-known principle that translates to "continuous improvement" and focuses on making small, incremental changes to achieve significant results over time. This philosophy has transformed industries, organizations, and personal lives by showing that consistent, gradual efforts can lead to remarkable progress. This applies in learning any skill, like playing the piano, coding, or painting.

Story of Team sky and their coach Dave Brailsford

The story begins with Team Sky, a professional cycling team from Great Britain with a history of mediocre performance. For over a century, they had never won a major cycling tournament, and prospects for change seemed bleak.

Then, they brought in Dave Brailsford, a British cycling coach who transformed the team's fortunes.

Brailsford introduced a straightforward yet powerful approach to performance enhancement, which he termed the "Theory of Marginal Gains." His strategy focused on making small, incremental improvements across various aspects of the team's operations.

The journey started with practical upgrades like using lighter bicycle tires and better seats. He also replaced outdoor suits with lighter indoor suits for racing. Brailsford meticulously measured and monitored the cyclists' conditions, continuously making adjustments to address their weakest areas.

But Brailsford's focus went beyond the obvious. He even experimented with different pillows to find the one that provided the best sleep for the riders and ensured improved hygiene practices to minimize the risk of infection.

Under Brailsford's leadership, British cyclists dominated, winning 59 World Championships across various disciplines from 2003 to 2013.

The story of Drew Carey

Drew Carey has been a prominent figure in the entertainment industry, famously known for his role on "The Drew Carey Show" as the overweight lead. His fans were stunned when he reappeared as the host of the show "The Price is Right," looking 80 pounds lighter. Carey's weight loss was not due to any quick-fix solution; he achieved it through traditional methods—by counting calories and dedicating 45 minutes each day to cardio on the treadmill.

You don't need to try the latest diet trends. Just find what works for you and stick with it. Over time, you will reach your goals.

Ask yourself,

1. Which skill can I focus on improving each day?

2. How much time should I dedicate to it each day?

3. What is one adjustment I need to make in my daily routine to enhance that skill?

The key points to remember from this chapter are,

- The power of small daily improvements in skill development, advocating for a focused approach where individuals enhance a specific skill regularly, leading to significant progress over time.
- Drawing from the Kaizen philosophy of continuous improvement, it highlights the success of Team Sky, whose achievements stemmed from making numerous minor adjustments.
- The journey of Drew Carey, who transformed his health through consistent effort rather than quick fixes.
- By having a growth mindset that values incremental progress and regularly monitoring growth, anyone can achieve mastery in their chosen skills and elevate their overall performance.

Worksheet: Work on Your Skill

1. Which skill can I focus on improving every day?

----

2. How much time should I dedicate to it every day?

----

3. What is one adjustment I need to make in my daily routine to enhance that skill?

CHAPTER 26:
LEARN SOMETHING NEW EVERY DAY

Learning is a treasure that will follow its owner everywhere.

— Chinese Proverb

Have you ever heard the saying, "You learn something new every day"? This happens when you observe how things are happening around you. But here I am not talking about the lessons you learn from nature or events. Instead, I am taking your attention that you must learn something new every day. It is not just a nice idea; it is actually a great way to make life more interesting and rewarding. Learning something new a little every day will make you more familiar with different things.

Learn three things every day. These three things must be very small. For example, if you are learning to improve your knowledge about the English language then:

- You can learn five English words to improve your vocabulary.
- You can learn to pronounce five sentences correctly.
- You can learn to write five sentences using five words you have learned.

Learning new thing not just enhances your knowledge but also boost your confidence.

Today we are in the digital age, and there's a variety of new skills to explore like video recording and editing, writing blogs, creating content, digital marketing, designing posters, learning new software etc.

You can watch educational videos or documentaries on different topics. You can also explore new subjects like artificial intelligence in various areas like, health, education, and technology etc. This can be a great way to broaden your knowledge and understand different fields. For me, listening to TED talks are great way to learn new ideas and different approaches towards different areas from science and technology to history and personal development.

Podcasts are also very popular now days. It covers a range of subjects that you are curious about. It can be a convenient way to learn while you are on the way to your office or college.

You can also read an interesting article daily. Whether it's fiction or non-fiction, reading regularly can expand your knowledge and imagination. There are so many areas like,

- Discover new music or art
- Experimenting with cooking
- Solving riddles, puzzles or problem-solving games
- Learning different activities like dance step, yoga poses etc.
- Watch content from different cultures

These activities can be integrated into your daily routine in a way that keeps learning enjoyable and engaging.

Ask yourself,

1. What new skill or subject do I want to learn today?
2. Can I identify five small things I can learn or explore today?
3. How can I incorporate learning into my daily routine?

The key takeaways from this chapter are,

- Making a commitment to learn something new every day can enhance your life and keep it interesting.
- Focus on learning three small things each day, such as: Five new English words to enhance vocabulary.
- Correct pronunciation of five sentences in any language.
- Writing five sentences using the words you've learned.
- Regular learning enhances knowledge and boosts confidence.
- Explore new skills relevant to the digital age, such as video editing, digital marketing, and content creation.

- Utilize educational videos, documentaries, and TED Talks to broaden your knowledge in various fields.

Worksheet: Learn Something New Every Day

1. What new skill or subject do I want to learn today?

---

2. Can I identify five small things I can learn or explore today?

---

3. How can I incorporate learning into my daily routine?

CHAPTER 27:
TRACK YOUR PROGRESS

Plan your progress carefully; hour-by-hour, day-by-day, month-by-month. Organized activity and maintained enthusiasm are the wellsprings of your power

— Paul J. Meyer

Tracking daily progress is a good source of motivation for achieving success. Be it a big project, learning a new skill, or building up a new habit—if you can keep track of your daily progress, then it will show you how far you've reached and where you need to head further.

Monitoring your progress ensures that you are motivated and channelled in the right direction while working on long-term projects or adopting some new habit after a personal goal. It is like traveling without a compass—you may get lost in the way and take more time to reach your destination.

First things first, you don't know what your progress is if you don't know what you're working toward. Set specific and clearly defined goals. For example, if you want to learn how to play the violin, one of your goals could be to practice playing for 30 minutes each day. Make sure your goals are achievable and measurable.

Take time weekly or monthly to reflect on where you are in this process. Consider what has been done and check if you are on track toward your goals. If you are not making the progress that you had hoped for, try to determine what the cause of this delay might be and make adjustments in your approach as needed.

Not every celebration has to happen when you reach your very last goal. You will want to celebrate steps along the way and allow yourself rewards for keeping yourself motivated and focused. Tracking progress sometimes indicates areas where one may be falling short. Try not to get too down, but instead, use that as an opportunity for improvement. Instead of getting discouraged, try to look at the setbacks as opportunities to learn from mistakes.

During my Ph.D. thesis, I committed to writing three pages every day for three months. I measured every day by keeping track in a diary. You must have a specific plan for anything to achieve. Without consistent effort and tracking your progress, no one can achieve significant success at any time in their life.

Measuring progress at the end of the day is crucial. Think about the battery indicator on your phone or laptop. If you did not have a way to see how much charge is left, you would not know when you need to recharge. In the same way, you can't measure how far you have come or what adjustments you might need to make.

What a true line by Peter Drucker, "You can't manage what you don't measure". If we you want to excel or improve in anything, start measuring it.

- You want to lose weight. Start measuring your weight, your calories intake, and the water you drink.
- You want to increase your wealth, start making a budget. Track every penny you spend and earn.
- You want to improve your life style. Just keep track of your daily activities.

Improving at something is a consistent effort. Anything improves or increases when we pay attention to it. If you pay attention to yourself every day, you will notice minute things about you like how you respond to daily tasks. How you spend your times and many more things.

How to measure progress

- Write a couple of lines each day about what you accomplished. It might just be about the time you worked on your goal or obstacles that you faced.
- Make a list of things to do to achieve your goal. Check them off as you go. This may be especially helpful in projects that require several steps.
- Many Apps are available that you can use to track daily progress and triggering reminders.
- Use a calendar mark down on it daily.

Ask Yourself,

1. What you want to measure in your life?
2. Which technique you want to adopt to measure?
3. What you need to change in your daily schedule?

The key points to remember from this chapter are,

- Tracking daily progress helps maintain motivation and shows how far you have come.
- It is useful for large projects, learning new skills, or building habits.
- Set specific, measurable goals (e.g., practice violin for 30 minutes daily).
- Regularly review your progress (weekly or monthly) to ensure you're on track and adjust as needed.
- Measuring progress is like checking a battery indicator—it shows when adjustments are needed.
- Creating and checking off a task list.
- Using calendar or apps for tracking and reminders.

Worksheet: Track Your Progress

1. What you want to measure in your life?

----

2. Which technique you want to adopt to measure?

----

3. What you needs to change in your daily schedule?

CHAPTER 28:
DO A LITTLE MORE

"The difference between ordinary and extraordinary is that little extra."

— Jimmy Johnson

In our busy lives, it might seem odd to think that doing just a little bit more can make a big difference. But the idea of "doing a little more" is really powerful. Small extra efforts can add up and lead to impressive results over time.

Every day, we tackle numerous tasks, each requiring time to complete. Among these, some tasks are especially important and need our full attention. These high-impact tasks, like exercising, reading, or fulfilling job responsibilities, can significantly affect our long-term well-being and success.

To manage these tasks effectively, start by making a list of them and prioritizing them based on their importance. Then, allocate specific time slots for each and put in a bit of extra effort.

For example, if you exercise in the morning or evening, try to walk a little further than usual or do one more push-up. When studying, extend your session by 10 minutes. By consistently doing a little more, you'll not only enhance your skills but also experience a sense of accomplishment and satisfaction. In your job, putting in a bit of extra effort can lead to greater success and fulfillment. Doing just a little more in each area of your life will help you feel more complete and happier.

The power of "Doing a little more" also comes from the compound effect. This means that small, regular actions can lead to significant results over time. For example, saving a little extra money each month can grow into a large amount thanks to interest.

In fitness, doing a few more exercises or eating a bit healthier each week can lead to big health improvements over time. The key is to keep making these small efforts regularly.

When I was in school, my father used to tell me to learna few English words every day. I used to write five words every day in a notebook.

In every area of life, there are something that

- You can do more
- Push yourself just a little
- Do it for more than five minutes

it's just not about the sports or physical exercises. It applies to everything we do.

- Reading few more pages
- More selfcare
- Little more work
- Extra efforts on your goal/work

Just remember this, high achievers do some extra. Extra can be anything. It can be a new skill that you want to add to your skill set but fail to do for so long. So, take a decision now to enroll into it.

Ask yourself,

1. In which areas of my life do I feel I could push myself just a little more?

2. How can I prioritize my tasks to ensure I focus on what matters most?

3. What small extra effort can I make today in my daily routine?

The key points to remember from this chapter are,

- Doing just a little more can make a big difference in many areas of life.

- By focusing on important tasks and adding small efforts, like exercising a bit longer or studying a few extra minutes, you can feel more accomplished and improve your skills over time.
- This idea connects to the compound effect, where small, regular actions add up to create significant results in health, money, and personal growth.
- Having a mindset of continuous improvement helps you stay motivated and satisfied. It reflects the habits of successful people leading to a more fulfilling life.

Worksheet: Do a Little More

1. In which areas of my life do I feel I could push myself just a little more?

----

2. How can I prioritize my tasks to ensure I focus on what matters most?

----

3. What small extra effort can I make today in my daily routine?

Kimdly scan the above QR Code for my youtuble channel.

Website: improvebitbybit.com

REFERENCES

https://prodiadigital.com/en/articles/benefits-of-30-minutes-daily-physical-activity-for-body-health

https://www.ncbi.nlm.nih.gov/pmc/articles/PMC6027933/?ref=healthtips.kr

Bedrov A, Bulaj G. Improving Self-Esteem With Motivational Quotes: Opportunities for Digital Health Technologies for People With Chronic Disorders. Front Psychol. 2018 Nov 2;9:2126. doi: 10.3389/fpsyg.2018.02126. PMID: 30450071; PMCID: PMC6224439.

Czuchry M., Dansereau D. F. (2005). Using motivational activities to facilitate treatment involvement and reduce risk. J. Psychoactive Drugs 37, 7–13. 10.1080/02791072.2005.10399744

https://explodingtopics.com/blog/smartphone-usage-stats

https://www.onlymyhealth.com/impact-of-excessive-screen-time-on-mental-health-and-how-to-manage-it-1695292936

Eime, R. M., Young, J. A., Harvey, J. T., Charity, M. J., & Payne, W. R. (2013). A systematic review of the psychological and social benefits of participation in sport for children and adolescents: informing development of a conceptual model of health through sport. *International journal of behavioral nutrition and physical activity*, *10*, 1-21.

https://www.activenorfolk.org/2021/05/mental-benefits-of-sport/

Hirshkowitz, M., Whiton, K., Albert, S. M., et al. (2015). National Sleep Foundation's sleep time duration recommendations: methodology and results summary. *Sleep Health*, 1(1), 40-43.

Walker, A. M. (2017). Why We Sleep: Unlocking the Power of Sleep and Dreams. Scribner.

Goel, N., Rao, H., Durmer, J. S., & Dinges, D. F. (2009). Neurocognitive consequences of sleep deprivation. *Seminars in Neurology*, 29(4), 320-339.

Cappuccio, F. P., D'Elia, L., Strazzullo, P., & Miller, M. A. (2010). Sleep duration predicts cardiovascular outcomes: a systematic review and meta-analysis of prospective studies. *Sleep*, 33(5), 605-614.

Roehrs, T., & Roth, T. (2001). Sleep, sleepiness, and alcohol use. *JAMA Psychiatry*, 58(5), 401-406.

https://www.edsys.in/motivational-stories-for-students/

Carrier, L. M., Rosen, L. D., Cheever, N. A., & Lim, A. F. (2015). Causes, effects, and practicalities of everyday multitasking. *Developmental review, 35*, 64-78.

Roberts, J. A., & David, M. E. (2016). My life has become a major distraction from my cell phone: Partner phubbing and relationship satisfaction among romantic partners. *Computers in human behavior, 54*, 134-141.

https://learningcenter.unc.edu/tips-and-tools/take-charge-of-distractions/

Kim, K. N. S., Lee, T. J., & Park, S. H. (2020). The impact of mobile phone notifications on working memory performance. ***Journal of Cognitive Psychology,** 32*(5), 415-425. doi:10.1080/20445911.2020.1782007

Harrison, M. R., & Clark, L. G. (2021). Distraction and its effects on cognitive performance: A review. ***Cognitive Research: Principles and Implications,** 6*(1), 12. doi:10.1186/s41235-021-00278-3

Baker, A. J., Smith, L. M., & Davis, R. C. (2022). The effect of multitasking on working memory and task performance: A meta-analysis. *Psychological Bulletin, 148*(6), 495-516. doi:10.1037/bul0000367

Lee, E. J., Nguyen, H. T., & Robinson, M. A. (2023). Effects of task switching and distraction on cognitive load and performance. *Journal of Experimental Psychology: Applied, 29*(3), 245-259. doi:10.1037/xap0000371

Thompson, R. S., Morales, J. W., & Green, C. P. (2024). Digital distractions and their impact on work efficiency: A longitudinal study. *Journal of Occupational Health Psychology, 29*(1), 58-73. doi:10.1037/ocp0000234

Keng, S. L., Smoski, M. J., & Robins, C. J. (2019). Effects of mindfulness on psychological health: A review of empirical studies. *Clinical Psychology Review, 33*(6), 643-652.

McEvoy, P. M., & Br partner, A. (2020). The role of overthinking in anxiety and depression: A review. *Journal of Anxiety Disorders, 73*, 102254.

Zhang, L., Zhou, Y., & Wang, S. (2021). The effects of mindfulness-based interventions on overthinking: A meta-analysis. *Mindfulness, 12*(1), 15-28.

Bavishi A, Slade M, Levy B. THE SURVIVAL ADVANTAGE OF READING BOOKS. *Innov Aging*. 2017;1(Suppl 1):477. Published 2017 Jun 30. doi:10.1093/geroni/igx004.1696

Stine-Morrow, Elizabeth A. L., et al. "The Effects of Sustained Literacy Engagement on Cognition and Sentence Processing among Older Adults." *Frontiers in Psychology*, vol. 13, 10 July 2022,

Mak HW, Fluharty M, Fancourt D. Predictors and impact of arts engagement during the COVID-19 pandemic: analyses of data from 19,384 adults in the COVID-19 Social Study. Front Psychol. 2021;12:626263. doi: 10.3389/fpsyg.2021.626263

Lewis, D. (2009), Galaxy Stress Research. Mindlab International, Sussex University, UK.

Rizzolo, D., Zipp, G. P., Stiskal, D., & Simpkins, S. (2009). Stress management strategies for students: The immediate effects of yoga, humor, and reading on stress. *Journal of College Teaching & Learning*, *6*(8), 79-88.

Koschwanez, Heidi E., et al. "Expressive writing and wound healing in older adults: a randomized controlled trial." *Psychosomatic Medicine* 75.6 (2013): 581-590.

Glass, O., Dreusicke, M., Evans, J., Bechard, E., & Wolever, R. Q. (2019). Expressive writing to improve resilience to trauma: A clinical feasibility trial. *Complementary therapies in clinical practice*, *34*, 240-246.

https://www.inc.com/marissa-levin/reading-habits-of-the-most-successful-leaders-that.html

Lally, P., Van Jaarsveld, C. H., Potts, H. W., & Wardle, J. (2010). How are habits formed: Modelling habit formation in the real world. *European journal of social psychology*, *40*(6), 998-1009.

https://www.successconsciousness.com/the-yogi-and-the-disciple/

Tugade MM, Fredrickson BL. Resilient individuals use positive emotions to bounce back from negative emotional experiences. J Pers Soc Psychol. 2004 Feb;86(2):320-33. doi: 10.1037/0022-3514.86.2.320. PMID: 14769087; PMCID: PMC3132556.

Fentaw, Y., Moges, B. T., & Ismail, S. M. (2022). Academic procrastination behavior among public university students. *Education Research International*, *2022*(1), 1277866.

https://studyblog.warwick.ac.uk/2022/03/31/combat-procrastination-right-now/

www.ingramcontent.com/pod-product-compliance
Lightning Source LLC
LaVergne TN
LVHW041611070526
838199LV00052B/3098